Mastering PHP Design Patterns

Develop robust and reusable code using a multitude of design patterns for PHP 7

Junade Ali

BIRMINGHAM - MUMBAI

Mastering PHP Design Patterns

First published: September 2016

Production reference: 1230916

Published by Packt Publishing Ltd.

Livery Place

35 Livery Street

Birmingham B3 2PB, UK.

ISBN 978-1-78588-713-0

www.packtpub.com

Credits

Author

Junade Ali

Reviewer

Sworup Shakya

Commissioning Editor

Kunal Parikh

Acquisition Editor

Chaitanya Nair

Content Development Editor

Nikhil Borkar

Technical Editor

Hussain Kanchwala

Copy Editor

Safis Editing

Project Coordinator

Suzanne Coutinho

Proofreader

Safis Editing

Indexer

Tejal Daruwale Soni

Production Coordinator

Aparna Bhagat

Cover Work

Aparna Bhagat

About the Author

Junade Ali was a technical lead at some of the UK's leading digital agencies and has also worked using PHP in mission-critical road-safety systems. He loves pushing PHP to its innovative limits. Having started his career as a web development apprentice, he still remains engaged in the academic computer science community.

Junade, an avid contributor to the PHP community, has also spoken at PHPTek and the Lead Developer Conference. In addition to this, Junade was interviewed by Cal Evans for Voices of the ElePHPant, and he has appeared on the PHP Roundtable. In this spirit, Junade is proud of his local PHP user group: PHPWarks. Currently, Junade works at CloudFlare as a polymath, and helps make the Internet more secure and faster.

Outside of development, Junade has an interest in law and political campaigns and is a published author on constitutional law.

About the Reviewer

Sworup Shakya has worked as a web developer for more than ten years. He started his career as a Flash ActionScript developer, before moving on to ASP.NET MVC, and finally to PHP. During his time as a developer, Sworup worked extensively with frameworks, be it ASP.NET MVC or AngularJS or Laravel. However, while he was working as an ActionScript developer, he had to create one, which gave him knowledge of design patterns and OOP concepts that has helped him improve in order to be able to work on the frameworks he had to work on later.

Sworup received his Bachelor of Information Technology degree from Purbanchal University in Nepal. He currently works with Zimris Technologies Nepal Pvt. Ltd., a subsidiary of Zimris, LLC, as a senior developer.

Sworup likes to keep on top of the current technologies, keeping an eye on StackOverflow, Laracasts forums, and occasional podcasts. He posts on these mediums whenever he can and is looking to start a technical blog documenting his experiences at `http://www.sworup.com.np`. You can reach him at `sworup.shakya@gmail.com`.

I would like to thank Suzanne Coutinho, Francina Pinto and Chaitanya Nair of Packt Publishing for giving me this opportunity and helping me through the review process. I would like to thank my friends, family and colleagues for their unconditional support.

www.PacktPub.com

For support files and downloads related to your book, please visit www.PacktPub.com.

Did you know that Packt offers eBook versions of every book published, with PDF and ePub files available? You can upgrade to the eBook version at www.PacktPub.com and as a print book customer, you are entitled to a discount on the eBook copy. Get in touch with us at service@packtpub.com for more details.

At www.PacktPub.com, you can also read a collection of free technical articles, sign up for a range of free newsletters and receive exclusive discounts and offers on Packt books and eBooks.

https://www.packtpub.com/mapt

Get the most in-demand software skills with Mapt. Mapt gives you full access to all Packt books and video courses, as well as industry-leading tools to help you plan your personal development and advance your career.

Why subscribe?

- Fully searchable across every book published by Packt
- Copy and paste, print, and bookmark content
- On demand and accessible via a web browser

Table of Contents

Preface

Have you ever been to a PHP conference? If not, I'd highly recommend it, it is the closest you can get to a living and breathing PHP community. A few weeks ago, I flew from London to St. Louis, Misouri, to speak at php[tek] (the PHP conference run by php[architect]). After the conference, there was a small tradition within the PHP community known as WurstCon. Essentially, hundreds of PHP conference attendees cram themselves into a small hot dog shop and host a hot dog convention, often to the complete surprise of the staff there. Likewise, community nights at PHP events are the warmest and most accepting community occasions you'll ever run into; the PHP community is surely one that other development language communities envy.

As of PHP 7, the PHP project has changed dramatically; but what I love, remains strong. The warmth you will feel at any PHP conference, the openness in the documentation, and adoption in the language. Yes, there are practices that are undoubtedly bad within PHP itself; however, think of what the PHP community has recently achieved, ranging from PHPUnit to Composer. Throughout this book, bear in mind the improvements in PHP 7, a few of which I'll share with you. The trajectory of the project is now certainly upwards, and let's not forget that this wasn't always true. The PHP community has learned its lessons from the past, whilst the language maintains the flexibility to write what is bad.

This book will seek to impart strong software engineering skills to you with the focus on implementing them in PHP. At the time of publishing this book, there is a certain void and a necessity for this kind of material. This book seeks to be the lighthouse that will not only demonstrate software design theory, but also seek to impart practical information of real value to improve the quality and maintainability of the code you write. This book leaves no stone unturned throughout the software development cycle and will seek to confront the reasons as to why the majority of software projects fail whilst also addressing design, redesign, and safeguard effective code.

This book goes beyond traditional design patterns as envisaged by the Gang of Four and details the practices that passionate PHP developers need to be successful as software engineers or leads on detailed PHP projects. This book will introduce you to the core knowledge required to understand project management techniques, why the majority software development projects fail, and why you can make yours a success.

Originally, I gave thought to writing a book on PHP when Mandi Rose, who I worked with previously, suggested I put together a book on the practices I've learned with PHP. Needless to say, at the time that suggestion was made, the best of my career was undoubtedly ahead of me; when the opportunity actually arose to write something like this, I felt I had learned dramatically more as time progressed. By no means should you see this book as the be-all and end-all of PHP practices; instead, you should use it to increase your knowledge base on PHP, but by no means limit it to this. In this book, I aim to give something, however small, back to the PHP community; after reading this book, I would encourage you to get stuck in and share what you've learned with others.

Later in this book, I will advocate Extreme Programming as a methodology and courage as a key value of this methodology. I will ask you to bear in mind the explanation of courage in The Values of Extreme Programming: "We will tell the truth about progress and estimates. We don't document excuses for failure because we plan to succeed. We don't fear anything because no one ever works alone. We will adapt to changes whenever they happen." This is, of course, some key advice we should all follow and seek to genuinely understand risks instead of cowering behind them. For many of us, the code we write during parts of our career is the highest expression of our labor. Indeed, the late nights turning into early mornings we spend debugging and developing are what ultimately allow us to demonstrate the fruits of our labor. In essence, as software engineers, the code we write defines who we are, as such we should be open to constantly refining and refactoring our processes, which is what this book aims to support you in doing. I am incredibly honored that you chose to allow me to help you to reach this end.

What this book covers

Chapter 1, *Why "Good PHP Developer" Isn't an Oxymoron*, introduces the concept of design patterns as recurring solutions to commonly arising problems.

Chapter 2, *Anti-Patterns*, introduces how patterns can lead to decidedly negative consequences.

Chapter 3, *Creational Design Patterns*, discusses Gang of Four design patterns, namely those surrounding object creation.

Chapter 4, *Structural Design Patterns*, covers how multiple classes and objects can be combined to deliver a clearer interface.

Chapter 5, *Behavioral Design Patterns*, explains how to increase the flexibility of communication between objects by identifying patterns that can help with communication between them.

Chapter 6, *Architectural Patterns*, revolves around resolving common issues related to the architecture of a web application/system, potentially outside the code base itself.

Chapter 7, *Refactoring*, shows how to redesign code that has already been written to improve maintainability.

Chapter 8, *How to Write Better Code*, covers a range of concepts that haven't been discussed elsewhere, and it also concludes with some advice for developers.

What you need for this book

An installation of PHP 7 will serve you well throughout this book. You should be prepared to alter your development environment as needed throughout this book; we will address the installation of various tools as we encounter them.

This book is not for the despairingly hostile or those who are passively antagonistic to approaching new software engineering principles. It is not for those who seek to be lone warriors, either. When altering a given code base, you must seek to improve the code of the entire code base and everyone who works on it. You must be willing to take personal responsibility of the code you write and not blame external factors. Code maintainability cannot be improved unilaterally on shared code bases; you must write your code with the intention of maintaining code quality for those who maintain it after you. Additionally, seek to go into this book with the mindset of being able to share what you've learned, whether it is with those in your teams, your user groups, or the larger PHP community. In other words, approach this book with the end in mind; approach this book with the stated aim of improving your code and those in the code base you maintain.

Who this book is for

This book is certainly aimed at the PHP developer looking to learn about the complete set of skills needed to be a software engineer, in particular, some lessons from software design; this book will seek to educate you on how your code can be made more extensible and easier to develop on. This book seeks to take your code beyond just being a bag of functions and classes, instead preferring well-designed, well-written, and well-tested code.

You will need a working knowledge of PHP and enough to build an application, but by no means do you have to be a total expert at everything in PHP; a working knowledge of the basics of software engineering will certainly give you a heads up.

You must encounter this book with an open mind and a willingness to have your preconceptions about software development challenged. This book will confront some truths about how you may be failing personally as a developer; it is vital that you approach this book with a willingness to take these principles onboard.

This book presents a set of software development patterns and principles that you can adopt. It is vital that you understand where these patterns should and shouldn't be applied; this will be explained throughout the book, especially in the last chapter.

A key tenet of reading this book is understanding what PHP is for and what it isn't. I expect you to enter this book understanding what problems you expect PHP to solve and what you expect to use other software development languages to solve.

Conventions

In this book, you will find a number of text styles that distinguish between different kinds of information. Here are some examples of these styles and an explanation of their meaning.

Code words in text, database table names, folder names, filenames, file extensions, pathnames, dummy URLs, user input, and Twitter handles are shown as follows: "The index.php file now yields this result".

A block of code is set as follows:

```php
<?php

abstract class Notifier
{
 protected $to;

 public function __construct(string $to)
 {
 $this->to = $to;
 }

 abstract public function validateTo(): bool;

 abstract public function sendNotification(): string;

}
```

Any command-line input or output is written as follows:

```
echo $richard->hasPaws;
```

New terms and **important words** are shown in bold. Words that you see on the screen, for example, in menus or dialog boxes, appear in the text like this: "direct your web browser to your chosen web server and you should see **Hello world!** pop up on screen."

 Warnings or important notes appear in a box like this.

 Tips and tricks appear like this.

Reader feedback

Feedback from our readers is always welcome. Let us know what you think about this book—what you liked or disliked. Reader feedback is important for us as it helps us develop titles that you will really get the most out of.

To send us general feedback, simply e-mail feedback@packtpub.com, and mention the book's title in the subject of your message.

If there is a topic that you have expertise in and you are interested in either writing or contributing to a book, see our author guide at www.packtpub.com/authors.

Customer support

Now that you are the proud owner of a Packt book, we have a number of things to help you to get the most from your purchase.

Downloading the example code

You can download the example code files for this book from your account at http://www.packtpub.com. If you purchased this book elsewhere, you can visit http://www.packtpub.com/support and register to have the files e-mailed directly to you.

You can download the code files by following these steps:

1. Log in or register to our website using your e-mail address and password.
2. Hover the mouse pointer on the **SUPPORT** tab at the top.
3. Click on **Code Downloads & Errata**.
4. Enter the name of the book in the **Search** box.
5. Select the book for which you're looking to download the code files.
6. Choose from the drop-down menu where you purchased this book from.
7. Click on **Code Download**.

You can also download the code files by clicking on the **Code Files** button on the book's webpage at the Packt Publishing website. This page can be accessed by entering the book's name in the **Search** box. Please note that you need to be logged in to your Packt account.

Once the file is downloaded, please make sure that you unzip or extract the folder using the latest version of:

- WinRAR / 7-Zip for Windows
- Zipeg / iZip / UnRarX for Mac
- 7-Zip / PeaZip for Linux

The code bundle for the book is also hosted on GitHub at `https://github.com/PacktPubl ishing/Mastering-PHP-Design-Patterns/`. We also have other code bundles from our rich catalog of books and videos available at `https://github.com/PacktPublishing/`. Check them out!

Errata

Although we have taken every care to ensure the accuracy of our content, mistakes do happen. If you find a mistake in one of our books—maybe a mistake in the text or the code—we would be grateful if you could report this to us. By doing so, you can save other readers from frustration and help us improve subsequent versions of this book. If you find any errata, please report them by visiting `http://www.packtpub.com/submit-errata`, selecting your book, clicking on the **Errata Submission Form** link, and entering the details of your errata. Once your errata are verified, your submission will be accepted and the errata will be uploaded to our website or added to any list of existing errata under the Errata section of that title.

To view the previously submitted errata, go to `https://www.packtpub.com/books/content/support` and enter the name of the book in the search field. The required information will appear under the **Errata** section.

Piracy

Piracy of copyrighted material on the Internet is an ongoing problem across all media. At Packt, we take the protection of our copyright and licenses very seriously. If you come across any illegal copies of our works in any form on the Internet, please provide us with the location address or website name immediately so that we can pursue a remedy.

Please contact us at `copyright@packtpub.com` with a link to the suspected pirated material.

We appreciate your help in protecting our authors and our ability to bring you valuable content.

Questions

If you have a problem with any aspect of this book, you can contact us at `questions@packtpub.com`, and we will do our best to address the problem.

1
Why "Good PHP Developer" Isn't an Oxymoron

Back in 2010, MailChimp published a post on their blog, entitled *Ewww, You Use PHP?* In this blog post, they described the horror when they explained their choice of PHP to developers who consider the phrase *good PHP programmer* an oxymoron. In their rebuttal they argued that their PHP wasn't *your grandfathers PHP* and that they use a sophisticated framework. I tend to judge the quality of PHP on the basis of, not only how it functions, but how secure it is and how it is architected. This book focuses on ideas of how you should architect your code. The design of software allows for developers to ease the extension of the code beyond its original purpose, in a bug-free and elegant fashion.

As Martin Fowler put it:

> *"Any fool can write code that a computer can understand. Good programmers write code that humans can understand."*

This isn't just limited to code style, but how developers architect and structure their code. I've encountered many developers with their noses constantly stuck in the documentation, copying and pasting bits of code until it works; hacking snippets together until it works. Moreover, I far too often see the software development process rapidly deteriorate as developers ever more tightly couple their classes with functions of ever increasing length.

Software engineers mustn't just code software; they must know how to design it. Indeed often a good software engineer, when interviewing other software engineers will ask questions about the design of the code itself. It is trivial to get a piece of code that will execute, and it is also benign to question a developer as to whether `strtolower` or `str2lower` is the correct name of a function (for the record, it's `strtolower`). Knowing the difference between a class and an object doesn't make you a competent developer; a better interview question would, for example, be how one could apply subtype polymorphism to a real software development challenge. Failure to assess software design skills dumbs down an interview and results in there being no way to differentiate between those who are good at it, and those who aren't. These advanced topics will be discussed throughout this book, by learning these tactics, you will better understand what the right questions to ask are when discussing software architecture.

Moxie Marlinspike once tweeted the following:

> *"As a software developer, I envy writers, musicians, and filmmakers. Unlike software, when they create something it is really done, forever".*

When developing software, we mustn't forget we are authors, not just of instructions for a machine, but we are also authoring something that we later expect others to extend upon. Therefore, our code mustn't just be targeted at machines, but humans also. Code isn't just poetry for a machine, it should be poetry for humans also.

This is, of course, better said than done. In PHP, this may be found especially difficult given the freedom PHP offers developers on how they may architect and structure their code. By the very nature of freedom, it may be both used and abused, so it is true with the freedom offered in PHP.

Therefore, it is increasingly important that developers understand proper software design practices to ensure their code maintains the long term maintainability. Indeed, another key skill lies in *refactoring* code, improving the design of existing code to make it easier to extend in the long term.

Technical debt, the eventual consequence of poor system design, is something that I've found comes with the career of a PHP developer. This has been true for me whether it has been dealing with systems that provide advanced functionality or simple websites. It usually arises because a developer elects to implement a bad design for a variety of reasons; this is when adding functionality to an existing codebase or taking poor design decisions during the initial construction of software. Refactoring can help us address these issues.

SensioLabs (the creators of the Symfony framework) have a tool called **Insight** that allows developers to calculate the technical debt in their own code. In 2011, they did an evaluation of technical debt in various projects using this tool; rather unsurprisingly they found that WordPress 4.1 topped the chart of all platforms they evaluated with them claiming it would take 20.1 years to resolve the technical debt that the project contains.

Those familiar with the WordPress core may not be surprised by this, but this issue of course is not only associated to WordPress. In my career of working with PHP, from working with security critical cryptography systems to working with systems that work with mission critical embedded systems, dealing with technical debt comes with the job. Dealing with technical debt is not something to be ashamed of for a PHP developer, indeed some may consider it courageous. Dealing with technical debt is no easy task, especially in the face of an ever more demanding user base, client, or project manager; constantly demanding more functionality without being familiar with the technical debt the project has associated to it.

I recently e-mailed the PHP Internals group as to whether they should consider deprecating the error suppression operator @. When any PHP function is prepended by an @ symbol, the function will suppress an error returned by it. This can be brutal, especially where that function renders a fatal error that stops the execution of the script, making debugging a tough task. If the error is suppressed, the script may fail to execute without providing developers a reason as to why this is. Usage of this operator may be described as an anti-pattern in some situations, something we will cover in `Chapter 4`, *Structural Design Patterns*.

Despite the fact that no one objected to the fact that there were better ways of handling errors (`try/catch`, `proper validation`) than abusing the error suppression operator and that deprecation should be an eventual aim of PHP, it is the case that some functions return needless warnings even though they already have a success/failure value. This means that due to technical debt in the PHP core itself, this operator cannot be deprecated until a lot of other prerequisite work is done. In the meantime, it is down to developers to decide the best methodologies of handling errors. Until the inherent problem of unnecessary error reporting is addressed, this operator cannot be deprecated. Therefore, it is down to developers to be educated as to the proper methodologies that should be used to address error handling and not to constantly resort to using an @ symbol.

Fundamentally, technical debt slows down development of a project and often leads to code being deployed that is broken as developers try and work on a fragile project.

When starting a new project, never be afraid to discuss architecture as architecture meetings are vital to developer collaboration; as one Scrum Master I've worked with said in the face of criticism that "meetings are a great alternative to work", he said "meetings are work…how much work would you be doing without meetings?".

In the rest of this chapter, we will cover the following points:

- Coding style – the PSR standards
- Revising object-oriented programming
- Setting up the environment with Composer

- Who are the Gang of Four?

Coding style – the PSR standards

When it comes to coding style, I would like to introduce you to the PSR standards created by the PHP Framework Interop Group. Namely, the two standards that apply to coding standards are PSR-1 (Basic Coding Style) and PSR-2 (Coding Style Guide). In addition to this, there are PSR standards that cover additional areas, for example, as of today; the PSR-4 standard is the most up-to-date autoloading standard published by the group. You can find out more about the standards at http://www.php-fig.org/.

Coding style being used to enforce consistency throughout a code base is something I strongly believe in. It does make a difference to your code readability throughout a project. It is especially important when you are starting a project (chances are you may be reading this book to find out how to do that right) as your coding style determines the style the developers following you in working on this project will adopt. Using a global standard such as PSR-1 or PSR-2 means that developers can easily switch between projects without having to reconfigure their code style in their IDE. Good code style can make formatting errors easier to spot. Needless to say that coding styles will develop as time progresses, to date I elect to work with the PSR standards.

I am a strong believer in the phrase: *always code as if the guy who ends up maintaining your code will be a violent psychopath who knows where you live*. It isn't known who wrote this phrase originally, but it's widely thought that it could have been John Woods or potentially Martin Golding.

I would strongly recommend familiarizing yourself with these standards before proceeding in this book.

Revising object-oriented programming

Object-oriented programming is more than just classes and objects; it's a whole programming paradigm based around *objects* (data structures) that contain data fields and methods. It is essential to understand this; using classes to organize a bunch of unrelated methods together is not object orientation.

Assuming you're aware of classes (and how to instantiate them), allow me to remind you of a few different bits and pieces.

Polymorphism

Polymorphism is a fairly long word for a fairly simple concept. Essentially, polymorphism means the same *interface* is used with a different underlying code. So multiple classes could have a draw function, each accepting the same arguments, but at an underlying level, the code is implemented differently.

In this section, I would like to talk about Subtype Polymorphism in particular (also known as Subtyping or Inclusion Polymorphism).

Let's say we have animals as our supertype; our subtypes may well be cats, dogs, and sheep.

In PHP, interfaces allow you to define a set of functionality that a class that implements it must contain, as of PHP 7 you can also use scalar type hints to define the return types we expect.

So for example, suppose we defined the following interface:

```
interface Animal
{
  public function eat(string $food) : bool;

  public function talk(bool $shout) : string;
}
```

We could then implement this interface in our own class, as follows:

```
class Cat implements Animal {
}
```

If we were to run this code without defining the classes we would get an error message as follows:

```
Class Cat contains 2 abstract methods and must therefore be declared
abstract or implement the remaining methods (Animal::eat, Animal::talk)
```

Essentially, we are required to implement the methods we defined in our interface, so now let's go ahead and create a class that implements these methods:

```
class Cat implements Animal
{
  public function eat(string $food): bool
  {
    if ($food === "tuna") {
      return true;
    } else {
```

```
        return false;
    }
  }

  public function talk(bool $shout): string
  {
    if ($shout === true) {
    return "MEOW!";
    } else {
    return "Meow.";
    }
  }
}
```

Now that we've implemented these methods, we can then just instantiate the class we are after and use the functions contained in it:

```
$felix = new Cat();
echo $felix->talk(false);
```

So where does polymorphism come into this? Suppose we had another class for a dog:

```
class Dog implements Animal
{
  public function eat(string $food): bool
  {
    if (($food === "dog food") || ($food === "meat")) {
    return true;
    } else {
    return false;
    }
  }

  public function talk(bool $shout): string
  {
    if ($shout === true) {
    return "WOOF!";
    } else {
    return "Woof woof.";
    }
  }
}
```

Now let's suppose we have multiple different types of animals in a pets array:

```
$pets = array(
  'felix'    => new Cat(),
  'oscar'    => new Dog(),
```

```
    'snowflake' => new Cat()
);
```

We can now actually go ahead and loop through all these pets individually in order to run the `talk` function. We don't care about the type of pet because the `talk` method that is implemented in every class we get is by virtue of us having extended the Animals interface.

So let's suppose we wanted to have all our animals run the `talk` method. We could just use the following code:

```
foreach ($pets as $pet) {
  echo $pet->talk(false);
}
```

No need for unnecessary `switch/case` blocks in order to wrap around our classes, we just use software design to make things easier for us in the long-term.

Abstract classes work in a similar way, except for the fact that abstract classes can contain functionality where interfaces cannot.

It is important to note that any class that defines one or more abstract classes must also be defined as abstract. You cannot have a normal class defining abstract methods, but you can have normal methods in abstract classes. Let's start off by refactoring our interface to be an abstract class:

```
abstract class Animal
{
  abstract public function eat(string $food) : bool;

  abstract public function talk(bool $shout) : string;

  public function walk(int $speed): bool {
    if ($speed > 0) {
      return true;
    } else {
      return false;
    }
  }
}
```

You might have noticed that I have also added a `walk` method as an ordinary, non-abstract method; this is a standard method that can be used or extended by any classes that inherit the parent abstract class. They already have their implementation.

Note that it is impossible to instantiate an abstract class (much like it's not possible to instantiate an interface). Instead, we must extend it.

So, in our `Cat` class let's remove the following:

```
class Cat implements Animal
```

We will replace it with the following code:

```
class Cat extends Animal
```

That's all we need to refactor in order to get classes to extend the `Animal` abstract class. We must implement the abstract functions in the classes as we outlined for the interfaces, plus we can use the ordinary functions without needing to implement them:

```
$whiskers = new Cat();
$whiskers->walk(1);
```

As of PHP 5.4 it has also become possible to instantiate a class and access a property of it in one system. PHP.net advertised it as: *Class member access on instantiation has been added, e.g. (new Foo)->bar().* You can also do it with individual properties, for example, `(new Cat)->legs`. In our example, we can use it as follows:

```
(new \IcyApril\ChapterOne\Cat())->walk(1);
```

Just to recap a few other points about how PHP implemented OOP, the `final` keyword before a class declaration or indeed a function declaration means that you cannot override such classes or functions after they've been defined.

So, let's try extending a class we have named as `final`:

```
final class Animal
{
  public function walk()
  {
    return "walking...";
  }
}

class Cat extends Animal
{
}
```

This results in the following output:

```
Fatal error: Class Cat may not inherit from final class (Animal)
```

Similarly, let's do the same except at a function level:

```
class Animal
{
```

```
  final public function walk()
  {
    return "walking...";
  }
}

class Cat extends Animal
{
  public function walk () {
    return "walking with tail wagging...";
  }
}
```

This results in the following output:

```
Fatal error: Cannot override final method Animal::walk()
```

Traits (multiple inheritance)

Traits were introduced in PHP as a mechanism for introducing Horizontal Reuse. PHP conventionally acts as a single inheritance language, because of the fact that you can't inherit more than one class into a script.

Traditional multiple inheritance is a controversial process that is often looked down upon by software engineers.

Let me give you an example of using Traits first hand; let's define an abstract `Animal` class that we want to extend into another class:

```
class Animal
{
  public function walk()
  {
    return "walking...";
  }
}

class Cat extends Animal
{
  public function walk () {
    return "walking with tail wagging...";
  }
}
```

So now let's suppose we have a function to name our class, but we don't want it to apply to all our classes that extend the `Animal` class, we want it to apply to certain classes irrespective of whether they inherit the properties of the abstract `Animal` class or not.

So we've defined our functions like so:

```
function setFirstName(string $name): bool
{
  $this->firstName = $name;
  return true;
}

function setLastName(string $name): bool
{
  $this->lastName = $name;
  return true;
}
```

The problem now is that there is no place we can put them without using Horizontal Reuse, apart from copying and pasting different bits of code or resorting to using conditional inheritance. This is where Traits come to the rescue; let's start off by wrapping these methods in a Trait called `Name`:

```
trait Name
{
  function setFirstName(string $name): bool
  {
    $this->firstName = $name;
    return true;
  }

  function setLastName(string $name): bool
  {
    $this->lastName = $name;
    return true;
  }
}
```

So now that we've defined our Trait, we can just tell PHP to use it in our `Cat` class:

```
class Cat extends Animal
{
  use Name;

  public function walk()
  {
    return "walking with tail wagging...";
```

```
  }
}
```

Notice the use of the `Name` statement? That's where the magic happens. Now you can call the functions in that Trait without any problems:

```
$whiskers = new Cat();
$whiskers->setFirstName('Paul');
echo $whiskers->firstName;
```

All put together, the new code block looks as follows:

```
trait Name
{
  function setFirstName(string $name): bool
  {
    $this->firstName = $name;
    return true;
  }

  function setLastName(string $name): bool
  {
    $this->lastName = $name;
    return true;
  }
}

class Animal
{
  public function walk()
  {
    return "walking...";
  }
}

class Cat extends Animal
{
  use Name;

  public function walk()
  {
    return "walking with tail wagging...";
  }
}

$whiskers = new Cat();
$whiskers->setFirstName('Paul');
echo $whiskers->firstName;
```

Scalar type hints

Let me take this opportunity to introduce you to a PHP 7 concept known as **scalar type hinting**; it allows you to define the return types (yes, I know this isn't strictly under the scope of OOP; deal with it).

Let's define a function, as follows:

```
function addNumbers (int $a, int $b): int
{
    return $a + $b;
}
```

Let's take a look at this function; firstly you will notice that before each of the arguments we define the type of variable we want to receive; in this case, it's int (or integer). Next up, you'll notice there's a bit of code after the function definition : int, which defines our return type so our function can only receive an integer.

If you don't provide the right type of variable as a function argument or don't return the right type of the variable from the function; you will get a TypeError exception. In strict mode, PHP will also throw a TypeError exception in the event that strict mode is enabled and you also provide the incorrect number of arguments.

It is also possible in PHP to define strict_types; let me explain why you might want to do this. Without strict_types, PHP will attempt to automatically convert a variable to the defined type in very limited circumstances. For example, if you pass a string containing solely numbers it will be converted to an integer, a string that's non-numeric, however, will result in a TypeError exception. Once you enable strict_types this all changes, you can no longer have this automatic casting behavior.

Taking our previous example, without strict_types, you could do the following:

```
echo addNumbers(5, "5.0");
```

Trying it again after enabling strict_types, you will find that PHP throws a TypeError exception.

This configuration only applies on an individual file basis, putting it before you include other files will not result in this configuration being inherited to those files. There are multiple benefits of why PHP chose to go down this route; they are listed very clearly in version 0.5.3 of the RFC that implemented scalar type hints called **PHP RFC: Scalar Type Declarations**. You can read about it by going to http://www.wiki.php.net (the wiki, not the main PHP website) and searching for scalar_type_hints_v5.

In order to enable it, make sure you put this as the very first statement in your PHP script:

```
declare(strict_types=1);
```

This will not work unless you define strict_types as the very first statement in a PHP script; no other usages of this definition are permitted. Indeed, if you try to define it later on, your script PHP will throw a fatal error.

Of course, in the interests of the rage-induced PHP core fanatic reading this book in its coffee stained form, I should mention that there are other valid types that can be used in type hinting. For example, PHP 5.1.0 introduced this with arrays and PHP 5.0.0 introduced the ability for a developer to do this with their own classes.

Let me give you a quick example of how this would work in practice, suppose we had an Address class:

```
class Address
{
  public $firstLine;
  public $postcode;
  public $country;

  public function __construct(string $firstLine, string $postcode, string
$country)
  {
    $this->firstLine = $firstLine;
    $this->postcode = $postcode;
    $this->country = $country;
  }
}
```

We can then type the hint of the Address class that we inject into a Customer class:

```
class Customer
{
  public $name;
  public $address;

  public function __construct($name, Address $address)
  {
    $this->name = $name;
    $this->address = $address;
  }
}
```

And this is how it all can come together:

```
$address = new Address('10 Downing Street', 'SW1A 2AA', 'UK');
$customer = new Customer('Davey Cameron', $address);
var_dump($customer);
```

Limiting debug access to private/protected properties

If you define a class which contains private or protected variables, you will notice an odd behavior if you were to `var_dump` the object of that class. You will notice that when you wrap the object in a `var_dump` it reveals all variables; be they protected, private, or public.

PHP treats `var_dump` as an internal debugging function, meaning all data becomes visible.

Fortunately, there is a workaround for this. PHP 5.6 introduced the `__debugInfo` magic method. Functions in classes preceded by a double underscore represent magic methods and have special functionality associated with them. Every time you try to `var_dump` an object that has the `__debugInfo` magic method set, the `var_dump` will be overridden with the result of that function call instead.

Let me show you how this works in practice, let's start by defining a class:

```
class Bear {
  private $hasPaws = true;
}
```

Let's instantiate this class:

```
$richard = new Bear();
```

Now, if we were to try and access the private variable that is `hasPaws`, we would get a fatal error:

```
echo $richard->hasPaws;
```

The preceding call would result in the following fatal error being thrown:

```
Fatal error: Cannot access private property Bear::$hasPaws
```

That is the expected output, we don't want a `private` property visible outside its object. That being said, if we wrap the object with a `var_dump` as follows:

```
var_dump($richard);
```

We would then get the following output:

```
object(Bear)#1 (1) {
   ["hasPaws":"Bear":private]=>
   bool(true)
}
```

As you can see, our `private` property is marked as `private`, but nevertheless it is visible. So how would we go about preventing this?

So, let's redefine our class as follows:

```
class Bear {
  private $hasPaws = true;
  public function __debugInfo () {
    return call_user_func('get_object_vars', $this);
  }
}
```

Now, after we instantiate our class and `var_dump` the resulting object, we get the following output:

```
object(Bear)#1 (0) {
  }
```

The script all put together looks like this now, you will notice I've added an extra `public` property called `growls`, which I have set to `true`:

```
<?php
class Bear {
  private $hasPaws = true;
  public $growls = true;
  public function __debugInfo () {
    return call_user_func('get_object_vars', $this);
  }
}
$richard = new Bear();
var_dump($richard);
```

If we were to `var_dump` this script (with both `public` and `private` property to play with), we would get the following output:

```
object(Bear)#1 (1) {
  ["growls"]=>
  bool(true)
}
```

As you can see, only the `public` property is visible. So what is the moral of the story from this little experiment? Firstly, that `var_dumps` exposes private and protected properties inside objects, and secondly, that this behavior can be overridden.

Setting up the environment with Composer

Composer is a dependency manager for PHP, strongly inspired by Node's NPM and Bundler. It has now become integral to multiple PHP projects, including Laravel and Symfony. Why it is useful for us, however, is that it contains autoload functionality that is compliant with the PSR-0 and PSR-4 standards. You can download and install Composer from `http://getcomposer.org`.

In order to install Composer globally on Mac OS X or Linux, first you can run the installer:

`curl -sS https://getcomposer.org/installer | php`

And then you can move Composer to install it globally:

`mv composer.phar /usr/local/bin/composer`

If the command preceding fails due to a permissions issue, rerun the command except putting `sudo` at the very start. You'll be asked to enter your password after you type the command, just enter it and hit *Enter*. Once you've installed Composer by following the preceding steps, you can run it simply by running the `composer` command.

In order to install Composer on Windows it is easiest to just run the installer on the Composer website; currently you can find it at:

`https://getcomposer.org/Composer-Setup.exe`.

Composer is fairly easy to update, just run this command:

`Composer self-update`

Composer works by using the configuration in a file called `composer.json`, where you can outline external dependencies and your autoloading style. Once Composer has installed dependencies listed in this file, it writes a `composer.lock` file that details the exact versions it has installed. When using version control it is important that you commit this file (alongside the `composer.json` file), don't add it to your `.gitignore` file if you're on Git. This is very important because the lock file details the exact version of a package that was installed at a particular time in your version control system. You can, however, exclude a directory called `vendor`, I'll explain what that does later.

Let's start off by creating a file called `composer.json` in our project directory. This file is structured in JSON, so let me just remind you of how JSON works:

- JSON consists of key/value pairs of data, think of it like a set of variables being defined in a file
- A key value pair is comma separated, for example, `"key" : "value"`
- Curly brackets hold objects
- Square brackets hold arrays
- Multiple pieces of data must be comma separated, without leaving a trailing comma at the end of the data
- Keys and values that include strings must be wrapped in quotes
- A backslash \ is the escape key

So now we can add the following markup to the `composer.json` file:

```
{
  "autoload": {
    "psr-4": {
      "IcyApril\\ChapterOne": "src/"
    }
  }
}
```

So let me explain what this file does; it tells Composer to `autoload` everything in the `src/` directory into the `IcyApril\ChapterOne` namespace using the PSR-4 standard.

So, the next step is to create our `src` directory where we include the code we want to autoload. Done that? Right, now let's open up our command line and move into the directory where we've put our `composer.json` file.

In order to install everything in the `composer.json` file in your project just run the `composer install` command. For subsequent updates, the `composer update` command will update to the latest versions of all dependencies as defined in `composer.json`. If you don't want to do this, though, there is an alternative; running the `composer dump-autoload` command will solely regenerate the list of the PSR-0/PSR-4 classes that need to be included in the project (for example, you add, delete, or rename some of your classes).

Now let me cover how you will actually go about creating a class. So, let's create an `src` directory in our project and in that `src` directory create a new class called `Book`. You can do this by creating a file called `Book.php`. In that file, add something like this:

```
<?php
namespace IcyApril\ChapterOne;
```

```
class Book
{
  public function __construct()
  {
    echo "Hello world!";
  }
}
```

This is a standard class, except we're just defining a constructor that will echo `Hello world!` when the class is instantiated.

As you may have noticed, we've followed a few naming conventions; firstly, the PSR-1 standard declares that class names must be declared in StudlyCaps. PSR-2 has a few extra requirements; to name a few: four spaces instead of a tab, one blank space after a namespace or use declarations, and placing brackets on new lines. It's definitely worth taking the time to read these standards if you haven't already. You might not agree with every standard, you might have a subjective preference to how you format your own code; my advice is to put these preferences aside for the greater good. Having code that is standardized by means of utilizing the PSR standards offers great advantages when collaborating on common code bases. The benefit of having an external standard, built by an organization such as the PHP-FIG group, is that you have your configuration pre-built into your IDE (for example, PHPStorm supports PSR-1/PSR-2 out of the box). Not only this but, when it comes to formatting arguments you have a concrete impartial document that outlines how things should be done, which is great for stopping religious code formatting arguments during code reviews.

Now that we've created the class we can go ahead and run the `composer dump-autoload` command in order to refresh our autoloader script.

So, we've configured our Composer autoloader and we've also got a test class to play around with, but the next question is how we can implement this. So, let's go ahead and implement this. In the same directory where we've implemented our `composer.json` file, let's add our `index.php` file.

The line after you put in your PHP opening tag, we need to pull in our autoloader script:

```
require_once('vendor/autoload.php');
```

Then we can instantiate our `Book` class:

```
new \IcyApril\ChapterOne\Book();
```

Set up your web server, point your document root to the folder we created, direct your web browser to your chosen web server and you should see **Hello world!** pop up on screen. Now you can take apart the code and play around with it.

The completed code sample is available alongside this book, so you can open it up and play around with it directly from there, just in case you need any help debugging your code.

Whether your classes are abstract classes or mere interfaces, when autoloading we treat them all as classes.

The Gang of Four (GoF)

The architect Christopher Alexander, who mentioned how patterns can be used to address common design issues, originally documented the concept. The idea came about from Alexander; he proposes that design issues can be documented rigorously, alongside their proposed solution. Design patterns have most notably been applied to resolving architectural issues in software design.

In Christopher Alexander's own words:

> *"The elements of this language are entities called patterns. Each pattern describes a problem that occurs over and over again in our environment, and then describes the core of the solution to that problem, in such a way that you can use this solution a million times over, without ever doing it the same way twice."*

Alexander wrote his own book, predating the Gang of Four called, *A Pattern Language*. In this book, Alexander created his own language, he coined the phrase *pattern language* to describe this; this language was formed from the building blocks of Architectural patterns. By utilizing these Architectural patterns the book proposes that ordinary people can use this language as a framework to improve their neighborhoods and towns.

One such pattern that is documented in the book is *Pattern 12*, known as the Community of 7000; the book documents this pattern by stating the following:

> *"Individuals have no effective voice in any community of more than 5,000-10,000 persons."*

By using problems such as this one with their documented solution; the book ultimately forms patterns, these patterns seek to act as the building blocks for making communities better.

As I mentioned, Alexander predated the Gang of Four; but his work was essential for sowing the seeds for software design patterns.

Now, let's turn directly on to the authors known as *The Gang of Four*.

Nope, we're not referring to the 1981 defectors from the British Labour party or an English post-punk band; but we are talking about the authors of a book called *Design Patterns: Elements of Reusable Object-Oriented Software*. This book has been highly influential in the realm of software development and is well known in the software engineering field.

In the first chapter of the book, the authors discuss object-oriented software development from their own personal experience; this includes arguing how software developers should program for an interface and not an implementation. This leads to code ultimately utilizing central functions of object-oriented programming.

It is a common misconception that the book contains only four design patterns, this isn't true; it covers 23 design patterns from three fundamental categories.

Let's cover what these categories are:

- Creational
- Structural
- Behavioral

So let's break each one of these down.

Creational design patterns

Creational design patterns concern the creation of objects themselves. Basic instantiation of classes without using a design pattern can result in needless complexity, but also in significant design problems.

The main usage of Creational design patterns is to separate the instantiation of a class from the usage of that instance. Failure to use Creational design patterns can mean your code is harder to understand and test.

Dependency injection

Dependency injection is the process whereby you can actually input dependencies that your application needs directly into the object itself.

John Munsch left an answer on Stack Overflow called *Dependency injection for five year olds*, this answer was republished in the book *Mark Seeman's Dependency Injection in .NET*:

When you go and get things out of the refrigerator for yourself, you can cause problems. You might leave the door open, you might get something Mommy or Daddy doesn't want you to have. You might even be looking for something we don't even have or which has expired.

What you should be doing is stating a need, "I need something to drink with lunch," and then we will make sure you have something when you sit down to eat.

When writing a class, it's natural to use other dependencies; perhaps a database model class. So with dependency injection, instead of a class having its database model created in itself, you can create it outside that object and inject it in. In short, we separate our client's behavior from our client's dependencies.

When thinking of dependency injection, let's outline the four separate roles involved:

- The service to be injected
- The client that depends on the service being injected
- The interface that determines how the client can use the service
- The injector that is responsible for instantiating the service and injecting it into the client

Structural design patterns

Structural design patterns are fairly easy to explain, they act as interconnectors between entities. It serves as a blueprint for how basic classes can be combined to form bigger entities, all Structural design patterns involve the interconnections between objects.

Behavioral design patterns

Behavioral design patterns work to explain how objects interact with each other; how they can send messages between each of the objects and how you can divide the steps of various tasks up among classes.

Structural patterns describe the static architecture of a design; Behavioral patterns are more fluid and describe a flowing process.

Architectural patterns

This is not strictly a *design pattern* (but the Gang of Four didn't cover Architectural patterns in their book); but it is incredibly relevant for PHP developers due to the web-oriented nature of PHP. Architectural patterns address various different constraints in computer systems through addressing performance limitations, high availability, and also minimization of business risk.

Most developers will be familiar with the Model-View-Controller architecture when it comes to web frameworks, more recently other architectures have started to emerge; for example, a microservices architecture works by a set of RESTful APIs that are independent and interconnected. Some people believe microservices move problems from the software development layer to the systems architecture layer. The opposite of microservices often referred to as a monolithic architecture, is where all the code is together in one application.

Summary

In this chapter, we revised some PHP principles, including OOP principles. We also revised some PHP syntax basics. We have seen how you can use Composer for dependency management in PHP. In addition to this, we also discussed PSR standards and how you can implement them in your own code to make your code more readable by others, and also comply with some other important standards (be they autoloading or HTTP messaging). Finally, we introduced design patterns and the Gang of Four with the history behind design patterns.

2
Anti-Patterns

Here's where we start on anti-patterns; before you get your hopes up thinking I'm about to tell you something amazing that will wonderfully streamline your code without using design patterns, I won't be doing that here (did I mention I'm great at crushing hopes and dreams?). Anti-patterns are, in short, things you don't want in your code.

Speaking of crushing hopes and dreams, should you ever have a junior developer, anti-patterns are also a great way of teaching methodologies that should be equally avoided. Learning anti-patterns also can boost the effectiveness of code reviews; instead of debating code quality on the basis of personal opinions, you can have an external source to consult on code quality.

Anti-patterns constitute a terrible method of resolving a recurring problem that is usually ineffective and risks being highly counterproductive. They can then create technical debt as developers must later struggle to refactor to resolve the initial problems but hopefully use a more resilient design pattern.

We all have encountered Spaghetti Code; one contract developer I worked with exclaimed to an ever more demanding product owner in the face of high technical debt: "There is so much spaghetti I might as well open a restaurant!" Spaghetti Code is where the control structure of a program is barely comprehensible as it is so tangled and over-complicated and it may be described as an anti-pattern. One of the major criticisms in PHP 5.3.0 was the implementation of goto operators in the language. Indeed, those critiquing their implementation claimed goto operators would provide yet another excuse for more Spaghetti Code in PHP.

Gotos were highly controversial in PHP, with someone even going as far to report it as a bug, stating: "PHP 5.3 includes goto. This is a problem. Seriously, PHP has made it this far without goto, why turn the language into a public menace?"

In addition to this, the submitter of the bug report listed the expected result as: "the world will end" and the actual result being "the world ended". Despite this, goto operators in PHP are heavily restricted so you can't just jump in and out of functions. Some people also argue that they are useful in finite state machines (essentially something with a binary output based on multiple inputs), but this is also controversial; so I shall allow you to make your own judgments about them.

You may well have experienced copy and paste programming, where whole blocks of code are copied and pasted in a program; this is yet another example of bad software design. In reality, developers should be designing their software to create generic solutions to problems instead of copying, refactoring, and pasting bits of code to fit a situation.

I will introduce this chapter with a section on why learning anti-patterns is important. During this chapter, I will discuss not only traditional anti-pattern-related software design but also anti-pattern-related web infrastructure and management styles. In addition to this, I want to discuss some PHP-specific anti-patterns, or flaws in PHP, which you may need to compensate for in your own code.

This book contains a dedicated chapter on refactoring towards the end; if the process of refactoring is of interest to you, this chapter will help lay the foundations of the ideas you might want to start thinking about; in addition to this, the chapters specific to design patterns may help you realize the code you might be eventually aiming for. In the chapter dedicated to refactoring, we will also cover some code smells, which can help you discover anti-patterns in codebases you're maintaining.

Why anti-patterns matter

Most programmers come from a background of adopting some form of anti-pattern until eventually realizing how it doesn't scale or doesn't work well. When I was 17 and in my first job as an apprentice developer, I would be whisked down to London Monday-to-Friday, somehow compressing my suit and my totally black clothing into a surprisingly miniscule suitcase, and would learn about software development. On Fridays, we were often released for a half-day at 12:00 but I would pre-book my company train tickets in the afternoon so I would spend my time in fast-food restaurants or coffee shops working on simple projects. Every week, when I came back and tried to scale one of these solutions I would realize new scalability issues and code quality issues. Of course, I had done development before, but these were largely dealing with either brand new incredibly short programming tasks, using pre-made frameworks or dealing with legacy code where the architecture had already been done (or, as I now realize, butchered with a severely blunt knife). This learning process of scaling my own code was great; I rapidly taught myself how to design software better. As humans, we often don't know enough about a topic to know how little we know (something incredibly true I've found with those who manage software developers but has never written any code themselves); while bearing this in mind, we should remember we are never above learning from our own mistakes. While this is incredibly important, teaching ourselves documented anti-patterns is also vital in order to learn from others mistakes.

I was once the technical lead and mentor for a developer who had the most down-right brutal treatment from learning from his mistakes. In the first appraisal I had with this developer, I was told by my HR counterpart that every time he'd made a mistake both the previous technical and HR leads dragged him into a meeting room to go through a formal disciplinary process. Both of these people had incredibly limited technical knowledge and also were completely incompetent at managing developers (so much so that they were the type of people who lived in their own bubble, clueless of how people worked in more successful environments and largely stuck in dead-end careers without the knowledge to ever do anything meaningful in their careers). By the time they left, this poor developers confidence had been crushed to such a point that he had no real career ambition in web and wasn't keen to learn. There's nothing wrong with being happy in your position. As a former boss of mine once said after I told him something incredibly personal, "ultimately, all that matters is that you're happy". Yes, it takes a lot of people to make the world go round, but as soon as you put yourself in a position where you are either mentoring or managing other developers you have an obligation to keep yourself ahead of the game. If you are a manager, you should know how to do your job effectively. The best people managers I've had have been those that possess a wealth of knowledge, keeping up to date with the latest and greatest in management methodologies the same way I like to keep up to date with the latest and greatest in the PHP core and community. Throughout the course of writing this book, my knowledge of project and people management has improved, but it still has a long way to go, and therefore I'd not take a job with such line management responsibilities without educating myself first. At the company I worked at, where there was effectively bullying as a management strategy, I once mentioned this to the head of department who responded by saying "we're not saying it's the best way of doing it"; if that's true, surely something should be done to fix this, for the sake of the business! This wasn't true in the entire business; other departments had a very different attitude, and indeed, the Technical Director once gave a tech talk about this very topic and the importance of knowing that you don't know. The CEO of the company started a similar conversation with me, saying how he knew he didn't know. Old practices die hard, but at least they have started sailing on the winds of change.

So other than ranting (I do love a good rant), why am I talking about this? My point is that your attitude matters. One of my favorite quotes on this subject is that "if you treat your developers like idiots, they will soon become idiots". Let me extend upon this by saying this:

- Bad performance in students is often a reflection of bad performance from teachers.
- Everyone makes mistakes, mistakes getting out control is the fault of idiotic behavior from managers, not developers.
- Idiots attract idiots. If you are an idiot in your body of subject knowledge, you will in turn likely recruit more idiots.
- If you operate a regime of fear in your workplace, you are an idiot and scared of being found out.
- If you don't know how little you know and you don't seek to effectively cure your own ignorance, you are an idiot.
- If you treat your developers like idiots, you are an idiot.

In short, learn how little you know and grow. It sounds brutal, but it's the truth. We are all ignorant, we cannot know everything. Effectively utilizing our own knowledge in association with the knowledge of others is vital to success. Recognizing our own ignorance is key to this. For example, last year I decided that my knowledge in fundamental computer science wasn't broad enough to cope with my own demand for it, or the demands of those I mentored; therefore, I decided to go off and do a part-time master's degree in computer science. The learning process has been great and taught me about fields in computer science I didn't know existed before.

Some software developers use other people's work, and yes, WordPress or Drupal development can give you a happy and productive career, but you will find the building and architecting things for yourself to be a great learning experience. Having worked in a traditional engineering environment, I have been won over to the view that a firm theoretical background in computer science is hugely beneficial for software engineers. Indeed, the body of knowledge required to understand the fundamentals of computer science is actually quite easy to pick up. Of course, in many ways, I am preaching to the converted; if you are reading this book you presumably understand the need for a deeper theoretical computer science knowledge base, but please don't read this book and stop actively learning. Continue to have a plan to progress your knowledge, seek to improve the information stored in that piece of protein that resides in our skulls.

It is often said that *"in the land of the blind, the one-eyed man is king"*; smaller development teams may often lack the basics when it comes to good software development (perhaps out of lack of necessity), and indeed, some larger development environments who become stuck in the past may end up in the same situation. In this regard, knowledge just becomes more precious and it becomes equally important for developers to be educated about software development.

Anti-patterns aren't just something your team can be taught to avoid; good software development needs a firm understanding of not only the programming language but also a theoretical understanding of software development is key.

Finally, let me just steal this quote from an article on SourceMaking:

> *"Architecture-driven software development is the most effective approach to building systems. Architecture-driven approaches are superior to requirements-driven, document-driven, and methodology-driven approaches. Projects often succeed in spite of methodology, not because of it."*

Rant(s) over. Let's cover some anti-patterns.

Not invented here syndrome

Cryptography can teach us a very important lesson about software; this is especially true about Kerckhoffs's principle. The principle states this:

> *"A cryptosystem should be secure even if everything about the system, except the key, is public knowledge."*

This was reformulated by Claude Shannon in a form known as Shannon's Maxim:

> *"One ought to design systems under the assumption that the enemy will immediately gain full familiarity with them".*

In layman's terms, in order to have a secure system, it shouldn't be secure just because no one knows how it's been implemented ("security through obscurity"). If you were to secure your money through obscurity, you'd bury it under a tree and hope no one would find it. Whereas, when you use a real security mechanism, such as putting your money in a safe in a bank, you can have every detail about the security system as public information, but providing the security system is truly secure, you would really only have to keep the key to the safe secret and every other detail could be public knowledge. If someone was to find the key to your safe, you only need change the combination, whereas if someone actually found where your money was buried under a tree, you would actually have to dig up the money and find somewhere else to put it.

Security that is only done through obscurity is a bad idea (that said, it's not always a bad idea). As you may be aware, when you store a password in a database you should use a one-way cryptographic algorithm known as a **hashing algorithm** to ensure that if the database is stolen no one can ever use the data in the database to find the user's original password. Of course, in reality, you shouldn't just hash a password, you should salt it and use an algorithm such as PBKDF2 or BCrypt, but this book isn't about password security.

The reality of the situation, however, is that sometimes, when developers actually do bother to hash passwords, they decide to create their own password hashing functions, functions that are easily reversible and are only secured by the obscurity of someone not knowing the algorithm. This is a perfect example of *not invented here* (*NIH*) syndrome; instead of a developer using a well-created password hashing library that is highly respected, they decide to create their own, pretending they are a cryptographer without understanding the security implications of such a decision.

Thankfully, PHP now makes it painlessly easy to hash your passwords; the `password_hash` function and `password_verify` function make this really easy with the `password_needs_rehash` function even telling you when the hash needs to be recalculated. Nevertheless, I digress.

So what actually is NIH syndrome? NIH syndrome is where a false sense of pride in an organization or individual developers own ability leads them to build their own solution instead of adopting superior third-party solutions. Reinventing the wheel isn't only costly, unnecessary, and can add needless overhead in maintenance; it can also be horribly insecure.

That said, where solutions are closed source and locked down, then it might be a good idea to avoid them. Doing so would also avoid vendor lock-in and restrictions on business flexibility.

NIH syndrome relies on the existing solutions being good and living up to expectations. Using third-party libraries is no excuse not to review their code quality.

Contributing to open source solutions is a great way to alleviate these issues. Room for improvement on an existing library? Fork it, propose an amendment to be merged in. No library that does the functionality you're after? Then you might want to consider writing your own library and publishing it.

I will finish this section by saying that the world has become heterogeneous; people are no longer looking for one technology stack to answer all their prayers; people are nowadays after the best tool for the job. It's worth thinking how you can utilize this fact for your own benefit.

Third-party dependencies with Composer

Composer makes it really easy to manage third-party dependencies. In Chapter 1, *Why "Good PHP Developer" Isn't an Oxymoron*, I briefly described how you can use Composer for autoloading. Big deal, autoloading has been supported as a core function since PHP 5.1.2, but the great thing about Composer is that you can also use it for dependency management. Composer can effectively go and fetch the dependencies you need using the version constraints you specify.

Let's start off the with the following composer.json file:

```
{
  "autoload": {
    "psr-4": {
      "IcyApril\\ChapterOne": "src/"
    }
  }
}
```

So let's pull in a dependency:

```
{
  "autoload": {
    "psr-4": {
      "IcyApril\\ChapterOne": "src/"
    }
  },
  "require": {
    "guzzlehttp/guzzle": "^6.1"
  }
}
```

Note that all we've done is add a require parameter where we specify which software we want. No manually pasting files into your project or root, or using sub-modules in Git, for that matter!

In this case, we pulled in Guzzle, an HTTP library for PHP.

Composer by default queries repositories from a central repository called **Packergist**, which aggregates packages you can install from their various version control systems (such as GitHub, BitBucket, or another repository host). If you like, Packergist acts as a kind of phone book that connects the requests for packages from Composer to code repositories.

That said, it's not just Packergist repositories that Composer supports. In the spirit of being open source, it supports repositories from a range of VCS systems (such as Git/SVN) regardless of where they are hosted.

Let's take the following `composer.json` file:

```json
{
  "autoload": {
    "psr-4": {
      "IcyApril\\ChapterTwo": "src/"
    }
  }
}
```

Let me demonstrate how you can include a repository from BitBucket without it being on Packergist:

```json
{
  "autoload": {
    "psr-4": {
      "IcyApril\\ChapterOne": "src/"
    }
  },
  "require": {
    "IcyApril/my-private-repo": "dev-master"
  },
  "repositories": [
    {
      "type": "vcs",
      "url": "git@bitbucket.org:IcyApril/my-private-repo.git"
    }
  ]
}
```

It's that easy! You literally just specify the repository you want to pull in from and Composer does the rest. It's just as easy with other version control systems:

```json
{
  "autoload": {
    "psr-4": {
      "IcyApril\\ChapterOne": "src/"
    }
```

```
  },
  "require": {
    "IcyApril/myLibrary": "@dev"
  },
  "repositories": [
    {
      "type": "vcs",
      "url": "http://svn.example.com/path/to/myLibrary"
    }
  ]
}
```

Rather cheekily, Composer can even support PEAR PHP repositories:

```
{
  "autoload": {
    "psr-4": {
      "IcyApril\\ChapterOne": "src/"
    }
  },
  "require": {
    "pear-pear2.php.net/PEAR2_Text_Markdown": "*",
    "pear-pear2/PEAR2_HTTP_Request": "*"
  },
  "repositories": [
    {
      "type": "pear",
      "url": "https://pear2.php.net"
    }
  ]
}
```

In order to update the dependencies after you've made changes to your `composer.json` file, just run `composer update`.

Note that you can't update external dependencies using just `composer dump-autoload`. The reason for this is that `dump-autoload` will solely update the class map of your autoloader. It will essentially update the list of classes it needs to autoload; it won't go and pull in new dependencies.

Occasionally, when using Composer and pulling in dependencies, Git may say you need to generate a GitHub authentication key. This is because if you have Git installed on your local machine, Composer will go ahead and pull in dependencies by cloning then via a version control system; however, occasionally, if it's clinging repositories from GitHub, you might come up against its rate limit. If this happens there is no need to panic. Composer will give you instructions on how to actually go ahead and get an API key so you can proceed without rate limiting.

An easy way to get around this issue is simply to generate a local SSH key and then put your public key into your GitHub account. That way, when you clone from GitHub to your local machine you won't face any rate limitations and you won't need to bother setting up an API key either.

In order to generate an SSH key on a Linux/Mac OS X machine, you can just use run the `ssh-keygen` command, which will create a public and private key you can use for SSH authentication, including with Github or BitBucket. These keys will (usually) be stored in the `~/.ssh` directory, noting the tilde (~ represents your home directory). Therefore, in order to get your key printed out into your Terminal window, run the `cat ~/.ssh/id_rsa.pub` command. Note that the `.pub` suffix indicates that `id_rsa.pub` is your public key that you can publically share. You must not share your private key, which is usually named just `id_rsa`. On Windows, you can use a GUI tool known as **PuttyGen** to generate public and private keys.

Once you've got your public and private keys, you can simply put them in GitHub by visiting the GitHub website and going to the SSH Keys page in the settings menu, paste in your key, and save it.

For subsequent updates, `composer update` will update to the latest versions of all dependencies as defined in `composer.json`. If you don't want to do this, though, there is an alternative; running Composer `dump-autoload` will solely regenerate the list of the PSR-0/PSR-4 classes that need to be included in the project (for example, you add, delete, or rename some of your classes).

Composer also supports private repositories, allowing you to effectively manage code reuse across multiple projects. Another key benefit is how Composer automatically generates a lock file that you can commit in with your projects. This allows you to effectively manage exactly which precise version of a dependency was installed at a particular point in time when you make a commit using your version control system.

Composer makes it easy and effective to manage third-party dependencies. Some crucial libraries are already available via Composer, such as PHPUnit, but there are also some other great libraries to make your life easier. Two of my favorite database libraries on Composer are Eloquent (a database ORM system from Laravel that you can find at `illuminate/database`) and Phinx (a database migration/seeding system that you can find at `robmorgan/phinx`). In addition to this, there are some great SDKs for various APIs that are available from Packergist (Google publishes some of its SDKs, and there are also some more specific ones, such as the Twilio SDK for sending SMS messages from your PHP app).

Composer allows you to specify dependencies for particular environments; suppose you only want to pull in PHPUnit on your development environments…that's not a problem!

God objects

God objects are a tempting consequence of bad software design and also badly implemented object orientation.

Essentially, a **God object** is an object with either too many methods or too many properties; essentially, it's a class that knows too much or does too much. The God object soon becomes tightly coupled to (referenced by) lots of other bits of code in the application.

So what's actually wrong with this? Well, in short, when you have one bit of code tied into every single other bit of code, you quickly find a maintenance disaster. If you adjust the logic for a method in a God object for one use case, you might find it having unintended consequences for another element.

In computer science, it is often a good idea to adopt a divide and conquer strategy. Often, big problems are just a set of little problems. By solving this set of little problems you can rapidly solve the overall problem. Objects should typically be self-contained; they should only know problems about themselves and also should only solve one set of problems, its own problems. Anything that isn't relevant to this aim doesn't belong in that class.

It can be argued that objects relating to physical objects should be instantiated, while those that don't should be abstract classes.

The flip side to God objects being an anti-pattern is when developing embedded systems. Embedded systems are used to process data on anything from a calculator to LED signage; they are small chips that are essentially self-contained computers and quite low cost. In this use case, with restricted computational power you can often find that programming elegance and maintainability become peripheral concerns. Slight performance increase and centralization of control can be more important, meaning using God objects can be somewhat sensible. Fortunately, PHP is incredibly seldom used to program embedded systems, so you are incredibly unlikely to find yourself in this particular situation.

The most effective way of dealing with these classes is to split them into separate classes manually.

Another anti-pattern, called *Fear of Adding Classes*, can also play a part in this, along with failing to mitigating it. This is where developers are reluctant to create necessary classes.

So, here's an example of a God class:

```php
<?php
class God
{
  public function getTime(): int
  {
    return time();
  }

  public function getYesterdayDate(): string
  {
    return date("F j, Y", time() - 60 * 60 * 24);
  }

  public function getDaysInMonth(): int
  {
    return cal_days_in_month(CAL_GREGORIAN, date('m'), date('Y'));
  }

  public function isCacheWritable(): bool
  {
    return is_writable(CACHE_FILE);
  }

  public function writeToCache($data): bool
  {
    return (file_put_contents(CACHE_FILE, $data) !== false);
  }

  public function whatIsThisClass(): string
  {
```

```
    return "Pure technical debt in the form of a God Class.";
  }
}
```

So, as you can see that in this class, we've basically combined lots of irrelevant methods. In order to fix this, we can split this class up into two sub-classes, one being a `Watch` class and the other being a `CacheManager` class.

Here is the `Watch` class; this class is simply intended to show us the time in various formats:

```php
<?php

class Watch
{
  public function getTime(): int
  {
    return time();
  }

  public function getYesterdayDate(): string
  {
    return date("F j, Y", time() - 60 * 60 * 24);
  }

  public function getDaysInMonth(): int
  {
    return cal_days_in_month(CAL_GREGORIAN, date('m'), date('Y'));
  }
}
```

And here is the `CacheManager` class; this class separates all the cache's functionality so it is entirely separate from the `Watch` class:

```php
<?php
class CacheManager
{
  public function isCacheWritable(): bool
  {
    return is_writable(CACHE_FILE);
  }

  public function writeToCache($data): bool
  {
    return (file_put_contents(CACHE_FILE, $data) !== false);
  }
}
```

Environment variables in PHP source

Far too often you come across a project on GitHub and you notice that the original developer has left in a `config.php` file that contains (in the best case) useless database information or (in the worst case) incredibly important API keys.

When these files aren't accidentally versioned they are often shoved in a `.gitignore` file with a sample file attached for developers to amend as they need. One example of a platform that does this is WordPress.

There are some minor improvements to this, such as putting core configuration in an XML file that is buried in some obscure document with plenty of irrelevant configuration.

I've found that there tend to be two good ways of managing environment variables in PHP. The first method involves putting them in a file on your `root` folder in a format such as YML and reading these variables as required.

The second way, which I personally prefer, is a method implemented by a library known as `dotenv`. Essentially, what happens is there is a `.env` file is created and put in the room of your project. In order to read configuration from this file, you just need to call the `env()` function. You can then add this file to your `.gitignore` file so that when you push from your development environment and pull to various other server configurations this process is made easier. In addition to this, you can specify environment variables at the web server level, thus ensuring an additional level of security and also making management far easier.

So, for example, if my .env file had a `DB_HOST` property, then I can access it using `env('DB_HOST');`.

If you do go down the `dotenv` route, be sure to make sure that your `.env` is not publically visible from the document root. Either keep it out of your public HTTP directory (for example, in the level above), or restrict access to it at a web server level (for example, restrict permissions, or if you're using Apache, use your `.htaccess` file to limit access to it).

At the time of writing, you can require this library by simply running the following command:

```
composer require vlucas/phpdotenv
```

Soft Code may often also be an anti-pattern that is adopted by using configuration files. This is where you start putting business logic in configuration files instead of source code; therefore, it is worth reminding yourself to consider when something really needs to be configuration oriented.

Singletons (and why you should be using dependency injection)

Singletons are classes which can only be instantiated once. You can effectively only have one object per `Singleton` class in an application. If you've never heard of Singletons before you may jump into the air thinking "Yes! I have a million and one use cases for this!" Well, please don't. Singletons are just terrible and can be effectively avoided.

So, a `Singleton` class in PHP looks something like this:

```php
<?php

class Singleton
{

  private static $instance;

  public static function getInstance()
  {
    if (null === static::$instance) {
      static::$instance = new static();
    }

    return static::$instance;
  }

  protected function __construct()
  {
  }

  private function __clone()
  {
  }


  private function __wakeup()
  {
  }
}
```

So here are the reasons why this should be avoided:

- They are inherently tightly coupled meaning they are difficult to test, for example using unit tests. They even maintain their state throughout the life cycle of the application.
- They violate the Single Responsibility Principle by controlling their own creation and life cycle.
- Fundamentally, it results in you hiding the dependencies of your application in a `global` instance. You can no longer effectively follow your dependencies around your code as you can't follow where they are injected as function arguments. They make it ineffective to find the dependency chain should you need to analyze it.

That said, some people argue they can be a valid solution to resource contention (where you need to only have a single instance of a resource and you need to manage that single resource).

Dependency injection

Dependency injection is the antidote to Singletons. So, suppose you have a class that is called `Transaction`. As a constructor of the class, it accepts parameters called `$creditCardNumber` and `$clientID`, so therefore we can construct the object as follows:

```
$order = new Transaction('1234 5678 9012 3456', 26);
```

Using dependency injection, we would instead pass in objects of `$creditCard` and `$client` which would be instances of classes for the credit card and client. If you are using an ORM, this could be a database model class:

```
$order = new Transaction($clientCreditCard, $client);
```

Database as IPC

At the time of writing, I'm currently over the Atlantic, on my way from London to San Francisco, which is probably a good thing as it means my neck is decisively out of the reach of some previous developers I've worked with.

Let me clear this up for you; your database isn't a message queuing system. You don't use it schedule jobs or queue up tasks to be completed. If you need something to do that, use a queuing system. Your database is for data...the clue is in the name; don't shove temporary messages in there.

There are many reasons why this is a bad idea. One major issue is the fact that in databases there is no real way to not enforce a policy by which you can guarantee that a double-read will not occur, and that is by utilizing row locks. This in turn, results in processes (either incoming out outgoing) being blocked, which in turn results in processing only being able to be done in a serial fashion.

Furthermore, in order to check if there is any work to do you end up essentially counting the rows of data in the database to see if there is work to do; you run this on a continuous basis. MySQL doesn't support push notifications; unlike PostgreSQL it doesn't have the NOTIFY command to pair with a LISTEN channel.

Also note that when you merge a job queue with a database table that stores real data, you also invalidate the cache every time you complete a job and update a flag, in turn making MySQL far slower.

In short, it results in your database performing worse and can force it to slow critical messages to a standstill. You must be careful not to turn your database into a job queue by having this functionality sneak up on you; instead, use the database exclusively for data, and bear this in mind when extending your database.

RabbitMQ provides an open source queuing system with some great PHP SDKs.

Auto-increment database IDs

Database auto-increment is something I find incredibly frustrating; pretty much every PHP/MySQL beginner tutorial teaches people to do this, but you really shouldn't.

I have got experience trying to shard auto-increment database IDs, and it's messy. Let's suppose you shard the database so the dataset over two database servers...how on earth can you expect someone to scale auto-increment IDs?

MySQL now even features a UUID function, allowing you to generate good IDs with strong entropy, meaning it also features a higher theoretical limit than auto-increment triggers on tables with an int data type.

In order to use the UUID function, the database table should ideally be a CHAR(20).

Cronjob imitating service

This one is a personal hatred of mine. A developer needs a service to run indefinitely, so they just enable a cronjob that never ends, or simply have a cronjob that operates incredibly frequently (such as once every few seconds).

A cronjob is a scheduled job that will run at a predetermined time. It's not something that operates services for you. Not only is this messy from an architectural perspective, but it scales horribly and becomes terrible to monitor.

A constantly processing task should be treated as a daemon and not as something that runs on the basis of a cronjob.

Monit is a tool in Linux systems that allows you to imitate services.

You can install Monit using the `apt-get` command:

```
sudo apt-get install monit
```

Once Monit is installed, you can add processes to its configuration file:

```
sudo nano /etc/monit/monitrc
```

Monit can then be started by running the `monit` command. It also has a `status` command so you can verify it is still running:

```
monit
monit status
```

You can learn more about Monit and find out how to configure it at `http://www.mmonit.com`. It is a highly valuable tool for every DevOps focused developer to have in their armory.

Software in place of architecture

Often, developers will seek to rectify a system's architectural issues at the software development level. While this has use cases, I am a huge fan of seeking to avoid this practice where it is not necessary. Moving issues from the software architecture layer to the infrastructure layer has its advantages.

For example, suppose you need to proxy a request for a particular URL endpoint off to another server. I believe this is best done at the web server level as opposed to writing a PHP proxy script. Apache and Nginx can both handle reverse proxying, but writing a library to do this may mean you come up against several unheard issues. Have you thought you that you'll handle `HTTP PUT/DELETE` requests? What about error handling? Assuming you nail your library, what about performance? Can a PHP proxy script really be faster than a web server level proxy, utilizing a web server written in a low-level systems engineering language? Surely one or two lines in your web server configuration is far easier to implement that an entire proxy script in PHP?

Here's an example of just how easy it is to create a proxy in a VirtualHost. The following configuration as an Apache VirtualHost will allow you to reroute everything from `test.local/api` to `api.local` (it's even easier in Nginx):

```
<VirtualHost *:80>
    ServerName test.local
    DocumentRoot /var/www/html/
    ProxyPass /api http://api.local
    ProxyPassReverse /api http://api.local
</VirtualHost>
```

This is far easier to maintain than thousands of lines of code in a PHP library that imitates something that is already available in the ProxyPass Apache module.

I've heard a criticism of microservices that they seek to move problems from the software development layer to the infrastructure layer, but are we really saying that that's always a bad thing?

Yes, software developers have a vested interest in doing things at the software development layer, but it is often worth educating yourself about the functionality you have available higher up the chain and seeing if that can rectify any issues you are having.

Think in terms of Occam's razor: the shortest solution is often the best, as it is translated literally "more things should not be used than are necessary."

Interface Bloat

I have come across multiple instances of people thinking they're doing great architecture but it turns out their efforts turn out to be counterproductive. Interface Bloat is a common consequence of this.

Once, when I discussed the importance of Interfaces when doing polymorphism in PHP with a Scrum Master, he responded by telling me about an environment he once worked in where there was an engineer who spent months developing interfaces and thought he was doing brilliant architecture work. Unfortunately, it turns out he wasn't doing great infrastructure work, he was guilty of implementing Interface Bloat.

Interface Bloat is, as the name suggests, is where an Interface is excessively bloated. An interface can be so bloated that it becomes practically impossible for a class to be implemented any other way.

Interfaces should be used sparingly; do you actually need an interface if the class is only ever going to be implemented once and once alone (and realistically, no one is never going to need to tamper with such code?). If so, you might want to consider avoiding an interface in such a situation.

Interfaces should not be used as a means of testing unit functionality. In that situation you really should be using unit testing, for example, via PHPUnit. Even so, unit testing should test how a unit functions as opposed to being used as a tool to ensure no one edits your code.

So, let me draw you to one implementation of Interface Bloat. Let's take a look at the `Pheanstalk` interface class in the Pheanstalk open source library (note I have stripped the comments to make it more readable):

```php
<?php

namespace Pheanstalk;

interface PheanstalkInterface
{
    const DEFAULT_PORT = 11300;
    const DEFAULT_DELAY = 0;
    const DEFAULT_PRIORITY = 1024;
    const DEFAULT_TTR = 60;
    const DEFAULT_TUBE = 'default';
    public function setConnection(Connection $connection);
    public function getConnection();
    public function bury($job, $priority = self::DEFAULT_PRIORITY);
    public function delete($job);
```

```
    public function ignore($tube);
    public function kick($max);
    public function kickJob($job);
    public function listTubes();
    public function listTubesWatched($askServer = false);
    public function listTubeUsed($askServer = false);
    public function pauseTube($tube, $delay);
    public function resumeTube($tube);
    public function peek($jobId);
    public function peekReady($tube = null);
    public function peekDelayed($tube = null);
    public function peekBuried($tube = null);
    public function put($data, $priority = self::DEFAULT_PRIORITY, $delay =
self::DEFAULT_DELAY, $ttr = self::DEFAULT_TTR);
    public function putInTube($tube, $data, $priority =
self::DEFAULT_PRIORITY, $delay = self::DEFAULT_DELAY, $ttr =
self::DEFAULT_TTR);
    public function release($job, $priority = self::DEFAULT_PRIORITY,
$delay = self::DEFAULT_DELAY);
    public function reserve($timeout = null);
    public function reserveFromTube($tube, $timeout = null);
    public function statsJob($job);
    public function statsTube($tube);
    public function stats();
    public function touch($job);
    public function useTube($tube);
    public function watch($tube);
    public function watchOnly($tube);
}
```

Yuck! Notice how even constants have been put in the implement, the one thing you might actually want to change. Clearly, this is an interface for a class that can only be implemented one way, making the Interface useless.

Interfaces provide a great degree of structure when writing object-oriented code; once implemented, they act as the guarantor that the methods in an interface have been implemented in a class that implements it.

However, like most good things, it can be a double-edged sword. Someone once gave me an incredibly naive argument against architecture design; they cited one of their previous co-workers who spent months simply writing incredibly detailed Interfaces and thought it was great architecture. In fact, he was committing Interface Bloat.

Interfaces should not be a way of enforcing implementation; indeed, there are examples of interfaces that result in someone being faced with the problem of not ever actually being able to implement an interface into a class any other way.

Interfaces shouldn't contain thousands of methods that reference internal operations of the class. They should be lightweight and considered a way of guaranteeing that when something is queried that it is definitely there.

There is an anti-pattern known as the **swiss army knife** (or **kitchen sink**) around the idea that people try to design interfaces to fit every possible use case of a class. This can cause debugging, documentation and maintenance difficulties.

Cart before the horse

Like most developers, I occasionally get bemused by some project management strategies; *putting the cart before the horse* is no exception.

Putting the cart before the horse is an anti-pattern under which features that never need to be built are architected, thus wasting time. The particular setting this annoys me is in technical meetings discussing a long-term technical plan where a project manager will discuss a feature and immediately demand the technical details of how this feature could be implemented.

Firstly, it's important to note that good developers should go away and have research time to come up with a solution. A developer is only made stronger by the ability to research their intended solution, to break out with their development team, to look online for other people facing similar issues, and then to come back with a unified, well-architected solution.

I spoke at the inaugural Lead Developer conference in London, and there was one quote that stood out to me from listening to others talking at the event. It was reused from an African proverb, but is especially true in software engineering contexts:

> *"If you want to go fast, go alone. If you want to go far, go together".*

Having spoken to managing directors and CEOs of various companies, they like to have a broad balance of personalities on their board of directors. A chief financial officer (CFO) may well be a ruthless perfectionist, only satisfied once all their figures are drop-dead perfect, whereas a chief operations officer may well be a fierce pragmatist when it comes to delivering on time. Such can be true in development teams; having a broad input of specialisms and personalities proposing ideas that are battled out to come up with a well-rounded solution can be beneficial for large decisions where a sole developer alone cannot be expected to make the decisions. Yes, you might want a filter or even say that only a small subsection of the development team may be relevant for one particular decision, but on the whole, your developers need the resources and time to make architectural decisions.

Furthermore, the best place to make such architectural decisions is when they are most relevant, when it is necessary that they should be made.

Flat Earthers are people who believe that the earth is a flat disc. When confronted with the concept of gravity, they instead claim gravity doesn't exist and state that this flat earth is instead simply moving upwards in space at a speed of 9.8 m/s. Confronted with further scientific theories they instead create their own illogically pieced together view of how the physical universe exists. Of course, such a theory is ridiculous. My point here is that you should base your decisions on sound computer science (e.g. published RFCs) instead of creating your own computer science on an ad-hoc basis.

Separation of development and operations

I have encountered development environments where developers are expressly forbidden from doing anything at all operational, where traditional development structure is relentlessly battered by the 21st-century web environment. There were caged job roles; you were either a developer or you looked after hosting. They had separate budgets, despite the fact both departments had a clear common destiny.

The result of this kind of setup was that developers and operations technicians never shared knowledge. By combining development and operations (DevOps, if you will) there is not only an effective boost in the quality of the work delivered through a shared knowledge base, but efficiency increases by empowering developers.

In the example I gave, when a site hosted on a company server was hacked or vandalized, all operations would do was restore from a backup. Combining development efforts into this mix not only resulted in vulnerabilities being patched, but also effective measures being put into hosting environments to rectify these issues (be they brute-force plugins or web application firewalls).

Excessive separation of development responsibilities

Development responsibilities being split too blatantly can be detrimental to a team.

Some separation is necessary. For example, teams working with **Internet of Things (IoT)** platforms cannot be expected to maintain a strong electronics engineering knowledge and a strong frontend web development knowledge. That said, developers should be expected to learn other skills they encounter and this can be assisted by encouraging knowledge sharing. Having multi-disciplined team members is not a business disadvantage, indeed it is an advantage.

Error suppression operator

The error suppression operator in PHP is a very dangerous tool indeed. Simply by putting an at symbol, @, in front of a statement, you can suppress any errors that result from it, including fatal errors that stop the execution of a script.

Unfortunately, this cannot necessarily be deprecated yet in PHP; having spoken to those in the PHP internals group, it is the case that there is a whole lot of prerequisite work that would need to be done first as some PHP functions do not have companion error functions to yield the error in the execution of a PHP script. As a result of this, the only way to show a non-fatal error that does not necessarily stop the execution of a script is to catch the error that is thrown during the operation of that particular function

The PHP core unfortunately, contains a considerable amount of technical debt in and of itself. Unfortunately, one thing that a good PHP developer should be good at is spotting technical debt in the PHP core itself. Indeed, Facebook tried to bypass this problem by rewriting the PHP core themselves and calling it **Hak**; I shall leave you to decide on whether you should consider adopting it or not.

One feature I have quite enjoyed in developing in Go (a systems language written by Google) is the fact you can do multiple return types (for example, you can return two values from one function). This has the added benefit of meaning that instead of having a companion function that will return the error message you can simply return any errors in a single function call.

Another thing I do like in Go is the fact that all warnings are treated as errors. You assign a variable, then don't use it? The program will fail to run (unless you assign a variable to an underscore, _, which is a null assignment operator meaning the variable will not be stored anywhere). Treating warnings as errors has the result of meaning that when a developer encounters an error, they know it's serious.

So yes, PHP can learn a lot from languages such as Go, but fundamentally, it is clear that there is also a lot of work that already needs to be done on the PHP core, and in addition to this, the PHP community may well need a culture shift to being more open and less political. **PHP RFC: Adopt Code Of Conduct** proposed that PHP should adopt a *Code of Practice*. Needless to say, if this is adopted in some form the PHP community should benefit.

Turning back to the issue at hand, error suppression operators should be avoided unless strictly necessary in the interest of making debugging far easier for developers.

Blind faith

Once when I was around 11 years old I was sitting in a physics lesson with a limited quantity of protractors and we were slowly passing them around in order to draw an angle. Being the devious short cutter that I was at such a young age, I decided not to wait and just trace a drawing someone else made. This was to the horror of my physics teacher at the time who stopped dead in his tracks and shouted "NO! PHYSICS IS ABOUT ACCURACY!"

He had a point and this is something that is also very true in the programming world.

To avoid *blind faith*, you should be aware of the following mistakes:

- Failure to check return types
- Failure to check your data models
- Assuming data within your database is correct or is in the format you expect it to be

Let's take this to a more extreme level; take this code:

```php
<?php

$isAdmin = false;
extract($_GET);

if ($isAdmin === true) {
  echo "Hey ".$name."; here, have some secret information!";
}
```

In the preceding code, there are two key mistakes. The first mistake is that we're directly extracting GET variables; we're importing remotely defined variables into the current symbol table, effectively allowing anyone to override any variables defined before the extract.

Also, there is obviously an XSS vulnerability in that we are returning a GET variable without sanitizing it.

So here's how we can make it better:

```php
<?php
```

```php
$isAdmin = false;

if ($isAdmin === true) {
    echo "Hey ".htmlspecialchars($_GET['name'])."; here, have some secret
information!";
}
```

Sequential coupling

Sequential coupling is where you create a class that has methods that must be called in a particular order. Method names that start with `init`, `begin`, or `start` may be indicative of this behavior; this may be indicative of an anti-pattern depending on the context. Sometimes, engineers use cars to explain abstract concepts, here I'll do the same.

For example, take the following class:

```php
<?php

class BadCar
{
  private $started = false;
  private $speed = 0;

  private $topSpeed = 125;

  /**
   * Starts car.
   * @return bool
   */
  public function startCar(): bool
  {
    $this->started = true;

    return $this->started;
  }

  /**
   * Changes speed, increments by 1 if $accelerate is true, else decrease
by 1.
   * @param $accelerate
   * @return bool
   * @throws Exception
   */
  public function changeSpeed(bool $accelerate): bool
  {
    if ($this->started !== true) {
```

```php
      throw new Exception('Car not started.');
    }

    if ($accelerate == true) {
      if ($this->speed > $this->topSpeed) {
        return false;
      } else {
        $this->speed++;
        return true;
      }
    } else {
      if ($this->speed <= 0) {
        return false;
      } else {
        $this->speed--;
        return true;
      }
    }
  }

  /**
   * Stops car.
   * @return bool
   * @throws Exception
   */
  public function stopCar(): bool
  {
    if ($this->started !== true) {
      throw new Exception('Car not started.');
    }

    $this->started = false;

    return true;
  }
}
```

As you may note, we have to run the startCar function before we can use any of the other functions, or an exception is thrown. Really, if you try to accelerate a car that is not started, it shouldn't do anything, but for the sake of argument I've changed it so that the car will simply start first. In the next example of stopping the car, I have changed the class so that the method will return false if you try to stop the car without it running first:

```php
<?php
class GoodCar
{
  private $started = false;
```

```php
    private $speed = 0;

    private $topSpeed = 125;

    /**
     * Starts car.
     * @return bool
     */
    public function startCar(): bool
    {
      $this->started = true;

      return $this->started;
    }

    /**
     * Changes speed, increments by 1 if $accelerate is true, else decrease
by 1.
     * @param bool $accelerate
     * @return bool
     */
    public function changeSpeed(bool $accelerate): bool
    {
      if ($this->started !== true) {
        $this->startCar();
      }

      if ($accelerate == true) {
        if ($this->speed > $this->topSpeed) {
          return false;
        } else {
          $this->speed++;
          return true;
        }
      } else {
        if ($this->speed <= 0) {
          return false;
        } else {
          $this->speed--;
          return true;
        }
      }
    }

    /**
     * Stops car.
     * @return bool
     */
```

```
public function stopCar(): bool
{
  if ($this->started !== true) {
    return false;
  }

  $this->started = false;

  return true;
}
}
```

The big rewrite

One temptation of developers is to rewrite an entire codebase. There are pros and cons for you to decide, and yes, it is often harder to read existing code than it is to write new code; but please do bear in mind that rewrites take time and can be hugely costly for your business.

Always bear in mind that the sum of your technical debt from any one project can never be greater than starting the project from scratch.

Maiz Lulkin wrote the following in a brilliant blog post:

> *"The problem of big rewrites is that they are a technical solution to a cultural problem."*

Big rewrites are horribly inefficient, especially when you simply cannot guarantee that developers will know any better now. Architecting the new system and migrating the data inside the deadlines can be a tall order.

In addition to this, deploying the big rewrite can be hugely problematic; deploying such a change to the entire codebase of an application can be lethal. Try to deploy code regularly in frequent intervals. Try to change one thing at a time.

Your software that exists is your existing specification. By building a rewrite, you are building code on the basis of legacy code.

Fortunately, there is an alternative; rapidly improving your current code base in cycles. There are three primary steps you can take to improve your code base:

- Tests (unit tests, behavioral tests, and so on)
- Service splitting
- Perfectly staged migrations

There is a chapter in this book dedicated to refactoring and how we can alter the design of legacy code.

Automated tests

You need tests; yes, automated tests can be slow to write, but they are crucial for ensuring things don't break when you rewrite or refactor them.

It is also mission-critical that your tests and development occur on an environment that is as close to production as possible. Small changes in web server software or database permissions can have disastrous consequences.

Using an automated deployment system such as Vagrant with Puppet or Docker can be a great solution.

When doing unit tests with PHPUnit and Composer, you can just include it in your `composer.json` file to pull it in:

```json
{
  "autoload": {
    "psr-4": {
      "IcyApril\\Example": "src/"
    }
  },
  "require": {
    "illuminate/database": "*",
    "phpunit/phpunit": "*",
    "robmorgan/phinx": "*"
  }
}
```

In addition to this, a `phpunit.xml` file may also be useful so that PHPUnit knows where the tests are, but also where the Composer autoloader is (so it can go ahead and pull in classes):

```xml
<?xml version="1.0" encoding="UTF-8"?>
<phpunit colors="true" bootstrap="./vendor/autoload.php">
  <testsuites>
    <testsuite name="Application Test Suite">
      <directory>./tests/</directory>
    </testsuite>
  </testsuites>
</phpunit>
```

You can then write tests as you normally would in PHPUnit, for example:

```php
<?php
class App extends PHPUnit_Framework_TestCase
{
  public function testApp()
  {
$this->assertTrue(true);
  }
}
```

Except, of course, you have the added benefit of being able to pull in PHP classes in your autoloader as you need them.

Not all tests need to be unit tests. Writing external test scripts to test APIs can be beneficial too. A tool called **Selenium** (http://www.seleniumhq.org) can even help you with browser automation.

Service splitting

Splitting your monolith into small independent loosely coupled services is a great way to reduce technical debt.

Large monolith applications which have technical debt rooting right into the core of the application can be problematic to deal with. Building on top of such unstable foundations can be tough to split up later. There is a solution, however; by building new functionality as independent services you can effectively build on a new core with a stable foundation, diverging from your old weak infrastructure. You can then intercommunicate this with the old monolith and such new services using a RESTful structure.

This structure allows you to continue developing new functionality while migrating to a new microservices architecture.

Martin Fowler proposed a system known as **Branch by Abstraction**, which allows you to make the large-scale change to systems in a gradual way, which allows you to continue to release while change is still being conducted.

The first step is to capture the interaction between one section of client code and its supplier; we can then change that section of the code so it all inter-communicates via an abstraction layer.

We then do this for interactions with the supplier. As we do this, we take the opportunity to improve unit test coverage. Once a supplier isn't in use at all, we can migrate the clients over to use the supplier instead and delete the old supplier.

Perfectly staged migrations

Splitting your monolith into small independent loosely coupled services is a great way to reduce technical debt, but in this process, you clearly add extra burden to the architectural level.

When migrating data or hosting environments, you might come across difficulties in this process. This is particularly true when the deployment process isn't repeated and is unique for each deployment (such as in environments that don't use Continuous Integration).

Using container technology such as Docker can allow you to better perform rapid application deployments, allowing you to deploy faster while also increasing portability and simplifying maintenance. Some people may find other technologies, such as Vagrant, more beneficial for them; regardless, there is a common factor in all these technologies: infrastructure as code.

Infrastructure as code is the process of managing and provisioning computing infrastructure through code instead of interactive configuration tools; however, what we are after here is even more basic than this. What we want is to be able to stage and test migrations of any kind before the fact and re-run the exact process when we perform the migration.

By scripting migrations, you can test them beforehand just like code. You can be sure when it's done on a live server instead of a staging server there's a reduced chance of any mistakes.

In addition to this, the migrations can later be used to reverse engineer the process should a factor in the deployment cause problems later, or so the justifications for decisions can be seen. It essentially acts as an artifact for the software deployment process.

Where possible, as many resources as possible should be available during this process; this includes those deploying the code, developers who put the project together, and in extreme cases, a communications individual to keep clients up to date. Those resources allow rapid debugging of those issues, but it is vital that an individual deploying the code takes the lead and orchestrates when these resources are required in order to prevent distractions.

Working to a formal pre-planned routine, while also allowing room to correct any issues, can often help make deployments as painless as possible.

Tester-Driven Development

This is a tongue-in-cheek reference to **Test-Driven Development (TDD)**. TDD is a software development strategy largely revolving around using development tests to drive implementation towards fulfilling the requirements.

Tester-Driven Development, however, is where the requirements are the shortcut and it becomes the case that the software team starts specifying the requirements through bug reports. Tester-Driven Development can also be referred to as **Bug-Driven Development** as it essentially results in bug reports being used to specify actions and features that developers should implement.

For example, a developer builds a tool to export data from a database to a spreadsheet. It works perfectly, but a tester still comes back and raises a ticket saying that there is a bug in the product; they say that it doesn't contain the ability to export to PDF. If this wasn't in the requirements it shouldn't be raised as a bug. And yes, you should have requirements.

QA teams and testers exist to verify that software meets the requirements. They do not exist to specify the requirements themselves.

Bloated optimization

Often, developers may trip over themselves trying to optimize their code or their design artifacts to a ridiculous extent, often before their code even performs basic functions, or even before any code has been created at all. This can rapidly perform issues in production.

In this section, I wish to discuss three anti-patterns specifically relating to this topic:

- Analysis paralysis
- Bikeshedding
- Premature optimization

Analysis paralysis

In short, this is where a strategy is over-analyzed to the point where progress is slowed down, or even stopped entirely in extreme cases. Not only can such solutions become obsolete rapidly, they can be made in under-educated circumstances, for example, in a meeting where an over-analytic boss tries to dig too deep into detail in advance without allowing their developers to actually do some research.

Over-analyzing a problem and seeking a perfect solution upfront just does not work; programmers should seek to refine their solution, not come up with the refined solution up front.

Bikeshedding

Essentially, this is where analysis paralysis can occur on the basis of some very trivial decisions, for example, the color of a log in page. The only fix that's required is to not waste time on trivial decisions. Avoid design by committee where possible as the majority of people, regardless of how good they think their design skills are, are largely incompetent at design.

Premature optimization

In this section, so far, I've largely beaten up project managers; no time to beat up developers. Often, developers will seek to optimize their code prematurely without having educated data-led conclusions to drive where and when optimizations should be made.

Writing clean and readable code is your first priority; then you can use some great profiling tools to determine where your bottlenecks are. XDebug and New Relic are just some of the tools that are good at this.

That said, there are some cases where optimization must be done, particularly on some long computational tasks where it can be mission-critical to reduce something from O(N2) time to O(N). This said, most simple PHP web apps will have no real need to use this consideration.

Uneducated manager syndrome

Has your manager ever built a web app themselves? I find that this is a fairly important characteristic for a manager to have. The same way a junior doctor will report to a doctor who has been through the process of being a junior doctor themselves, or a teacher will report to a head teacher who themselves has been a teacher, a software developer should report to someone who has been through that process themselves.

Obviously, in small teams (for example, a small design house that does web development on the side), an engineering manager might not be strictly necessary. This works well where managers do understand the need to defer decisions to the programmers where necessary. However, as soon as things scale up, there needs to be structure.

Decisions such as who to hire, who to fire, how to address technical debt, which elements need most focus, and so on, need to be taken by developers; in addition to this, they sometimes mustn't be taken democratically because doing so would result in design by committee. In this instance, an engineering manager is required.

In large scale teams, there should always be a developer who spends more than 90% of their time not writing code.

I will take this a step further; a web engineering manager shouldn't just have a technical background, they should have a web background. Developing a Java application developer can be wholly different to building a PHP web application, and such an engineering manager should accordingly have an understanding of such a discipline by having some web experience (though it doesn't necessarily have to be in one particular language).

Wrong rocky foundations

The SensioLabs Insight tool was used to evaluate technical debt within various projects, and they evaluated and published the responses. SensioLabs responded on their blog saying that the results didn't account for project age or project size, but nevertheless it does show the technical debt you're up against in using some frameworks as foundations:

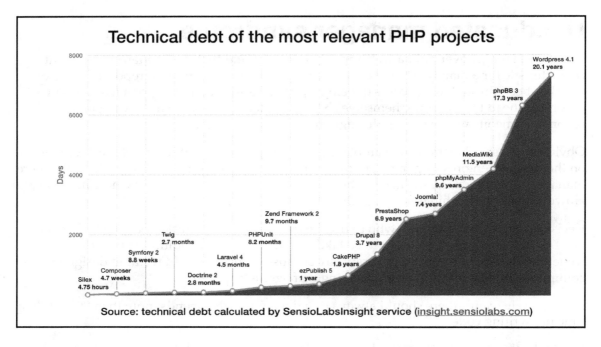

Don't get me wrong: WordPress is a great CMS; yes, it has some quirks in the core and comes from the days before OOP, but it's a great blogging platform. You ordinarily shouldn't be fiddling with it's core code, so you don't need to worry about it. By no means should you write your own blogging platform or CMS, but at the same time, WordPress isn't the right problem for building a marketing asset system or an insurance quote generator (yes, both are real projects I have been asked to do in WordPress initially).

In short: use the best foundations for your task.

Long methods

Methods can be overly complicated in some instances with PHP; for example, in the following class I have intentionally left out some meaningful comments and also made the constructor excessively long:

```php
<?php
class TaxiMeter
{
  const MIN_RATE = 2.50;
  const secondsInDay = 60 * 60 * 24;
  const MILE_RATE = 0.2;
```

```php
  private $timeOfDay;
  private $baseRate;
  private $miles;
  private $dob;

  /**
   * TaxiMeter constructor.
   * @param int $timeOfDay
   * @param float $baseRate
   * @param string $driverDateOfBirth
   * @throws Exception
   */
  public function __construct(int $timeOfDay, float $baseRate, string
$driverDateOfBirth)
  {
    if ($timeOfDay > self::SECONDS_IN_DAY) {
      throw new Exception('There can only be ' . self::SECONDS_IN_DAY . '
seconds in a day.');
    } else if ($timeOfDay < 0) {
      throw new Exception('Value cannot be negative.');
    } else {
      $this->timeOfDay = $timeOfDay;
    }

    if ($baseRate < self::MIN_RATE) {
      throw new Exception('Base rate below minimum.');
    } else {
      $this->baseRate = $baseRate;
    }

    $dateArr = explode('/', $driverDateOfBirth);
    if (count($dateArr) == 3) {
      if ((checkdate($dateArr[0], $dateArr[1], $dateArr[2])) !== true) {
        throw new Exception('Invalid date, please use mm/dd/yyyy.');
      }
    } else {
      throw new Exception('Invalid date formatting, please use simple
mm/dd/yyyy.');
    }
    $this->dob = $driverDateOfBirth;

    $this->miles = 0;


  }

  /**
   * @param int $miles
```

```
   * @return bool
   */
  public function addMilage(int $miles): bool
  {
    $this->miles += $miles;
    return true;
  }

  /**
   * @return float
   * @throws Exception
   */
  public function getRate(): float
  {
    $dynamicRate = $this->miles * self::MILE_RATE;

    $totalRate = $dynamicRate + $this->baseRate;

    if (is_numeric($totalRate)) {
      return $totalRate;
    } else {
      throw new Exception('Invalid rate output.');
    }
  }
}
```

Now, let's make just two small changes; let's extract some of our methods into their own functions and let's add some DocBlock comments. This is still by no means perfect, but note the difference that is made:

```
<?php

class TaxiMeter
{
  const MIN_RATE = 2.50;
  const SECONDS_IN_DAY = 60 * 60 * 24;
  const MILE_RATE = 0.2;

  private $timeOfDay;
  private $baseRate;
  private $miles;

  /**
   * TaxiMeter constructor.
   * @param int $timeOfDay
   * @param float $baseRate
   * @param string $driverDateOfBirth
   * @throws Exception
```

```php
    */
    public function __construct(int $timeOfDay, float $baseRate, string
$driverDateOfBirth)
    {
        $this->setTimeOfDay($timeOfDay);

        $this->setBaseRate($baseRate);

        $this->validateDriverDateOfBirth($driverDateOfBirth);

        $this->miles = 0;

    }

    /**
     * Set timeOfDay class variable.
     * Only providing it doesn't exceed the maximum seconds in a day (const
secondsInDay) and is greater than 0.
     * @param $timeOfDay
     * @return bool
     * @throws Exception
     */
    private function setTimeOfDay($timeOfDay): bool
    {
        if ($timeOfDay > self::SECONDS_IN_DAY) {
            throw new Exception('There can only be ' . self::SECONDS_IN_DAY . '
seconds in a day.');
        } else if ($timeOfDay < 0) {
            throw new Exception('Value cannot be negative.');
        } else {
            $this->timeOfDay = $timeOfDay;
            return true;
        }
    }

    /**
     * Sets the base rate variable providing it's over the MIN_RATE class
constant.
     * @param $baseRate
     * @return bool
     * @throws Exception
     */
    private function setBaseRate($baseRate): bool
    {
        if ($baseRate < self::MIN_RATE) {
            throw new Exception('Base rate below minimum.');
        } else {
            $this->baseRate = $baseRate;
```

```php
        return true;
    }
}

/**
 * Validates
 * @param $driverDateOfBirth
 * @return bool
 * @throws Exception
 */
private function validateDriverDateOfBirth($driverDateOfBirth): bool
{
    $dateArr = explode('/', $driverDateOfBirth);
    if (count($dateArr) == 3) {
        if ((checkdate($dateArr[0], $dateArr[1], $dateArr[2])) !== true) {
            throw new Exception('Invalid date, please use mm/dd/yyyy.');
        }
    } else {
        throw new Exception('Invalid date formatting, please use simple
mm/dd/yyyy.');
    }

    return true;
}

/**
 * Adds given milage to the milage class variable.
 * @param int $miles
 * @return bool
 */
public function addMilage(int $miles): bool
{
    $this->miles += $miles;
    return true;
}

/**
 * Calculates rate of trip.
 * Times class constant mileRate against the current milage in miles
class variables and adds the base rate.
 * @return float
 * @throws Exception
 */
public function getRate(): float
{
    $dynamicRate = $this->miles * self::MILE_RATE;

    $totalRate = $dynamicRate + $this->baseRate;
```

```
    if (is_numeric($totalRate)) {
      return $totalRate;
    } else {
      throw new Exception('Invalid rate output.');
    }
  }
}
```

Long methods are an indicator of code smell; they refer to a symptom in the code that may have its origins in a deeper problem. Other examples include duplicate code and contrived complexity (using advanced design patterns where a simpler approach would suffice).

Magic numbers

Note how in the preceding example I always put my constant numeric variables in class constants, as opposed to directly putting them in the code itself:

```
const minRate = 2.50;
const secondsInDay = 60 * 60 * 24;
const mileRate = 0.2;
```

The reason I did this was to avoid an anti-pattern known as **magic numbers** or **unnamed numerical constants**. Using class constants makes code easier to read, understand, and maintain; and of course, under the PSR standards, they should be declared in uppercase, separated by underscores.

Summary

In this chapter we covered some fundamental anti-patterns for you to avoid; some were architectural, some were PHP-related, and others were at the management layer.

Fundamentally, anti-patterns result in technical debt. By technical debt, we are talking about code that is so hard to extend that it becomes harder to make changes to later on.

Here's a list of things I want you to do to fix this:

- Plan before you start coding
- Make comments, and add a comment where the purpose of your code isn't immediately apparent
- Make sure your code has structure
- Try to avoid putting too much code in one method

- Use DocBlocking
- Use common sense approaches to PHP

In this chapter, we have learned some common design issues that can lead to severe problems; these principles can help you prevent sizable issues later on. Writing code to scale is an important factor of design. At its core, this requires understanding the constraints. Using proper strategies for inter-process communication can help your service scale while writing loosely coupled code can increase code reuse and debugging. Finally, when it comes to deploying this awesome code, automated testing and Perfectly Staged Migrations can make sure this goes off without a hitch.

In the next chapters, we will move on to covering some design patterns (presumably, what you've been waiting for).

If you are interested in learning about how to improve the design of an existing codebase, you might find the dedicated chapter on refactoring in this book particularly interesting; but it's worth reading up on the other design patterns first in order to gain an understanding of the patterns we are trying to refactor towards.

3
Creational Design Patterns

Creational design patterns are one of the three types of design pattern commonly associated with the Gang of Four; they are design patterns that concern object creation mechanisms.

Instantiating objects or basic class creation on their own, without controlling this process, can result in design problems or simply add additional complexity to the process.

In this chapter, we will cover the following topics:

- The software design process
- Simple Factory
- Factory Method
- Abstract Factory pattern
- Lazy initialization
- Builder pattern
- Prototype pattern

Before we learn about Creational design patterns, let's talk a little about the architectural process.

Software design process

Software Engineering Body of Knowledge is a book published by the *IEEE* often known as the **SWEBoK,** and it summarizes the generally accepted body of knowledge for the entire field of software engineering.

In this book, it is stated that the definition of software design is as follows:

"The process of defining the architecture, components, interfaces, and other characteristics of a system or component" and "the result of [that] process".

Specifically, software design can be split into two levels of hierarchy:

- Architectural design, describing how software is split into its composite components
- Detailed design, describing the specifics of each component in sufficient detail as to describe its component.

A component is a part of a software solution, with interfaces reaching off the component as both *required interfaces* (things the software requires to function) and *provided interfaces* (things the software provides to other components).

These two design processes (Architectural design and Detailed design) should result in a set of models and artifacts that record major decisions, with an explanation of why non-trivial decisions have been made. In the future, developers may then readily reference these documents in order to work out the rationale behind architectural decisions, making code more maintainable by ensuring decisions are thought through, and that thought process is passed down.

The first of these processes, Architectural design, can be fairly creative and engaging for an entire group. The outcome of this process, however you choose to do it, should be a component diagram that interconnects components together by their interfaces.

This process usually can favor groups of general developers instead of tiger teams. *Tiger teams* are usually small groups of a specialist in a particular domain of product knowledge, who come together in a time-boxed environment to address a particular issue under the chairmanship of an architect. Often, especially where legacy is involved, such design efforts may require a wide body of knowledge to extract the necessary architectural constraints.

This said, in order to prevent the process turning into the design by committee or mob rule there are some ground rules that you might want to follow: have an architect chair the meeting and work from the component level diagram without drilling any further. It often helps to mock up a component diagram before the meeting and to edit it as needed in the meeting itself, which helps ensure the team remains on track to correcting the diagram without drilling into the hows.

In one environment I have been in, there was a very detailed engineer who was head of the engineering team; he insisted on doing architecture by immediately drilling into the detail of components, which would rapidly leave the process disintegrated and unorganized; he would be starting *meetings in meetings* on the fly. Building component diagrams in these architecture meetings proved vital in keeping order in the meetings and ensuring both operational matters and Detailed design matters were not engaged with too early. Operational matters of how and where something is hosted is not usually within the remit of software engineering unless it directly has to alter how software is created.

The next step is Detailed design; this explains how a component is constructed. Design patterns used in construction, class diagrams and the necessary external resources can all be decided at this point. Some Detailed design work will be done at the construction level, regardless of how good the design is, software developers will need to make minor changes to the design to either add more detail or to flesh out some oversights in the architecture process. The process that is prior to this design must simply specify the component in sufficient detail to facilitate its construction and allow developers to not have to consider the architecture in too much detail. Developers should be developing code from artifacts that are closely related to the code (for example, Detailed designs) as opposed to coding from high-level requirements, designs, or plans.

As an aside, let's remember that unit tests can form part of the design (for example, when utilizing Test-Driven Development), with each unit test specifying a design element (classes, methods, and specific behavior). While it simply isn't realistic (though some will claim it is) to reverse engineer the code into the design artifacts; it is possible to represent *architecture as code*, if you will; unit tests are one such way of achieving this.

As mentioned earlier in this book, design patterns provide a crucial role in software design; they allow the design of more complicated bits of software without re-inventing the wheel.

Right; now to Creational design patterns.

Simple Factory

What is a factory? Let's imagine you order a new car; the dealer sends your order off to the factory and the factory builds your car. Your car is sent to you in its assembled form and you don't need to care about how it was made.

Similarly, a software factory produces objects for you. The factory takes your request, assembles the object using the constructor and gives them back to you to use. One of these types of Factory pattern is known as the **Simple Factory**. Let me show you how it works.

Firstly, we define an abstract class, which we want to extend with other classes:

```php
<?php

abstract class Notifier
{
  protected $to;

  public function __construct(string $to)
  {
    $this->to = $to;
  }

  abstract public function validateTo(): bool;

  abstract public function sendNotification(): string;

}
```

This class serves to allow us to have common methods and define whatever common functionality we want all the classes we build in our factory to have in common. We could also use interfaces instead of abstract classes for the implementation without defining any functionality whatsoever.

Using this interface, we can build two notifiers, SMS and Email.

The SMS notifier is as follows in the SMS.php file:

```php
<?php

class SMS extends Notifier
{
  public function validateTo(): bool
  {
    $pattern = '/^(\+44\s?7\d{3}|\(?07\d{3}\)?)\s?\d{3}\s?\d{3}$/';
    $isPhone = preg_match($pattern, $this->to);

    return $isPhone ? true : false;

  }

  public function sendNotification(): string
  {
```

```php
    if ($this->validateTo() === false) {
      throw new Exception("Invalid phone number.");
    }

    $notificationType = get_class($this);
    return "This is a " . $notificationType . " to " . $this->to . ".";
  }
}
```

Similarly, let's put out `Email` notifier in the `Email.php` file:

```php
<?php

class Email extends Notifier
{

  private $from;

  public function __construct($to, $from)
  {
    parent::__construct($to);

    if (isset($from)) {
      $this->from = $from;
    } else {
      $this->from = "Anonymous";
    }
  }

  public function validateTo(): bool
  {
    $isEmail = filter_var($this->to, FILTER_VALIDATE_EMAIL);

    return $isEmail ? true : false;

  }

  public function sendNotification(): string
  {
    if ($this->validateTo() === false) {
      throw new Exception("Invalid email address.");
    }

    $notificationType = get_class($this);
    return "This is a " . $notificationType . " to " . $this->to . " from "
. $this->from . ".";
  }
}
```

We can build our factory as follows:

```php
<?php

class NotifierFactory
{
  public static function getNotifier($notifier, $to)
  {

    if (empty($notifier)) {
      throw new Exception("No notifier passed.");
    }

    switch ($notifier) {
      case 'SMS':
        return new SMS($to);
        break;
      case 'Email':
        return new Email($to, 'Junade');
        break;
      default:
        throw new Exception("Notifier invalid.");
        break;
    }
  }
}
```

While we would ordinarily use Composer to do autoloading, in order to demonstrate how simple this method is, I will manually include the dependencies; so without further ado, here's our demo:

```php
<?php

require_once('Notifier.php');
require_once('NotifierFactory.php');

require_once('SMS.php');
$mobile = NotifierFactory::getNotifier("SMS", "07111111111");
echo $mobile->sendNotification();

require_once('Email.php');
$email = NotifierFactory::getNotifier("Email", "test@example.com");
echo $email->sendNotification();
```

We should get an output like this:

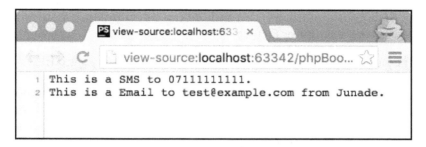

Factory Method

The Factory Method differs from the ordinary Simple Factory on the basis that instead of us having one factory, we can have many.

So why would you want to do this? Well, in order to understand this, we must look to the open/closed principle (OCP). Bertrand Meyer is usually associated with having originated the term *open/closed principle* in his book, *Object-oriented Software Construction*. Meyer stated the following:

> *"software entities (classes, modules, functions, etc.) should be open for extension, but closed for modification"*

Where a software entity needs to be extended, this should be possible without modifying its source code. Those of you who are familiar with the **SOLID** (**single responsibility**, **open-closed**, **Liskov substitution**, **interface segregation** and **dependency inversion**) principles of object-oriented software may already have heard of this principle.

The Factory Method allows you to group certain classes together and deal with them by means of an individual factory for a group of classes. If you want to add another group, you can just add another factory.

So now, how do we do this? Well, essentially we are going to create an interface for each factory (or an abstract method for that matter); we then implement that interface into any other factories we want to build.

So let's clone our Simple Factory demo; what we're going to do is make our
`NotifierFactory` become an interface. Then we can rebuild factories to have one factory
for electronic notifications (e-mail or SMS) and we can then implement our interface to
create, say, a postal courier notifier factory.

So let's start off by creating the interface in the `NotifierFactory.php` file:

```php
<?php

interface NotifierFactory
{
  public static function getNotifier($notifier, $to);
}
```

Now let's build our `ElectronicNotifierFactory` that implements our
`NotifierFactory` interface:

```php
<?php

class ElectronicNotifierFactory implements NotifierFactory
{
  public static function getNotifier($notifier, $to)
  {

    if (empty($notifier)) {
      throw new Exception("No notifier passed.");
    }

    switch ($notifier) {
      case 'SMS':
        return new SMS($to);
        break;
      case 'Email':
        return new Email($to, 'Junade');
        break;
      default:
        throw new Exception("Notifier invalid.");
        break;
    }
  }
}
```

We can now refactor our `index.php` to use the new factory we have made:

```php
<?php

require_once('Notifier.php');
```

```php
require_once('NotifierFactory.php');
require_once('ElectronicNotifierFactory.php');

require_once('SMS.php');
$mobile = ElectronicNotifierFactory::getNotifier("SMS", "07111111111");
echo $mobile->sendNotification();

echo "\n";

require_once('Email.php');
$email = ElectronicNotifierFactory::getNotifier("Email",
"test@example.com");
echo $email->sendNotification();
```

This now gives the same output as before:

```
This is a SMS to 07111111111.
This is a Email to test@example.com from Junade.
```

However, the benefit now is that we can now add a new type of notifier without ever needing to open the factory at all, so let's add a new notifier for postal communications:

```php
<?php

class Post extends Notifier
{
  public function validateTo(): bool
  {
    $address = explode(',', $this->to);
    if (count($address) !== 2) {
      return false;
    }

    return true;
  }

  public function sendNotification(): string
  {

    if ($this->validateTo() === false) {
      throw new Exception("Invalid address.");
    }

    $notificationType = get_class($this);
    return "This is a " . $notificationType . " to " . $this->to . ".";
  }
}
```

Then we can introduce the `CourierNotifierFactory`:

```php
<?php

class CourierNotifierFactory implements NotifierFactory
{
  public static function getNotifier($notifier, $to)
  {

    if (empty($notifier)) {
      throw new Exception("No notifier passed.");
    }

    switch ($notifier) {
      case 'Post':
        return new Post($to);
        break;
      default:
        throw new Exception("Notifier invalid.");
        break;
    }
  }
}
```

Finally, we can now amend our `index.php` file to include this new format:

```php
<?php

require_once('Notifier.php');
require_once('NotifierFactory.php');
require_once('ElectronicNotifierFactory.php');

require_once('SMS.php');
$mobile = ElectronicNotifierFactory::getNotifier("SMS", "07111111111");
echo $mobile->sendNotification();

echo "\n";

require_once('Email.php');
$email = ElectronicNotifierFactory::getNotifier("Email",
"test@example.com");
echo $email->sendNotification();

echo "\n";

require_once('CourierNotifierFactory.php');

require_once('Post.php');
```

```
$post = CourierNotifierFactory::getNotifier("Post", "10 Downing Street,
SW1A 2AA");
echo $post->sendNotification();
```

The `index.php` file now yields this result:

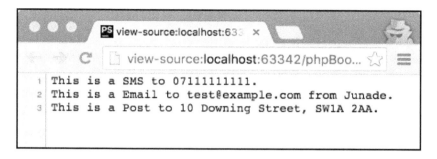

In production, you would generally put your notifiers in a different namespace alongside having your Factories in a different namespace.

Abstract Factory pattern

First, if you've done any background reading before approaching this book, you will have heard the phrase *concrete class*. What does this mean? Well, simply put, it is the opposite of an abstract class; it is a class you can instantiate to make an object.

An Abstract Factory consists of the following classes: an Abstract Factory, Concrete Factory, Abstract Product, Concrete Product, and our client.

In the Factory pattern, we produced implementations of a particular interface (for example, `notifier` was our interface and e-mail, SMS and post were our implementations). With an Abstract Factory pattern, we will create implementations of a factory interface, with every factory knowing how to create their products.

Suppose we have two toy factories, one in San Francisco and one in London. They both know how to create both company's products for both locations.

With this in mind, our `ToyFactory` interface looks like this:

```php
<?php

interface ToyFactory {
  function makeMaze();
  function makePuzzle();
}
```

Now that this is done, we can build our San Francisco toy factory (`SFToyFactory`) to serve as our Concrete Factory:

```php
<?php

class SFToyFactory implements ToyFactory
{
  private $location = "San Francisco";

  public function makeMaze()
  {
    return new Toys\SFMazeToy();
  }

  public function makePuzzle()
  {
    return new Toys\SFPuzzleToy;
  }
}
```

Now we can add our British toy factory (`UKToyFactory`):

```php
<?php

class UKToyFactory implements ToyFactory
{
  private $location = "United Kingdom";

  public function makeMaze()
  {
    return new Toys\UKMazeToy;
  }

  public function makePuzzle()
  {
    return new Toys\UKPuzzleToy;
  }
}
```

As you notice, we are creating various toys within the Toys namespace, so now we can put together our abstract methods for our toys. Let's start with our `Toy` class. Every toy will eventually extend this class:

```php
<?php

namespace Toys;

abstract class Toy
{
  abstract public function getSize(): int;
  abstract public function getPictureName(): string;
}
```

Now, for the two types of toy we declared in our `ToyFactory` interface at the start (maze and puzzle), we can declare their abstract methods, starting with our `Maze` class:

```php
<?php

namespace Toys;

abstract class MazeToy extends Toy
{
  private $type = "Maze";
}
```

Now let's do our `Puzzle` class:

```php
<?php

namespace Toys;

abstract class PuzzleToy extends Toy
{
  private $type = "Puzzle";
}
```

Now it's time for our concrete classes, so let's start with our implementations for San Francisco.

The code for `SFMazeToy` is as follows:

```php
<?php

namespace Toys;


class SFMazeToy extends MazeToy
{
  private $size;
  private $pictureName;

  public function __construct()
  {
    $this->size = 9;
    $this->pictureName = "San Francisco Maze";
  }

  public function getSize(): int
  {
    return $this->size;
  }

  public function getPictureName(): string
  {
    return $this->pictureName;
  }
}
```

And here's the code for the `SFPuzzleToy` class, a different implementation to the `Maze` toy' class:

```php
<?php

namespace Toys;


class SFPuzzleToy extends PuzzleToy
{
  private $size;
  private $pictureName;

  public function __construct()
  {
    $rand = rand(1, 3);

    switch ($rand) {
      case 1:
```

```
      $this->size = 3;
      break;
    case 2:
      $this->size = 6;
      break;
    case 3:
      $this->size = 9;
      break;
  }

  $this->pictureName = "San Francisco Puzzle";
}

public
function getSize(): int
{
  return $this->size;
}

public function getPictureName(): string
{
  return $this->pictureName;
}
}
```

We can now finish this off with our implementations for the British factory.

Let's start off by making one for the maze toy, UKMazeToy.php:

```
<?php

namespace Toys;


class UKMazeToy extends Toy
{
  private $size;
  private $pictureName;

  public function __construct()
  {
    $this->size = 9;
    $this->pictureName = "London Maze";
  }

  public function getSize(): int
  {
    return $this->size;
```

```
  }

  public function getPictureName(): string
  {
    return $this->pictureName;
  }
}
```

And let's make a class for the puzzle toy too, `UKPuzzleToy.php`:

```php
<?php

namespace Toys;


class UKPuzzleToy extends PuzzleToy
{
  private $size;
  private $pictureName;

  public function __construct()
  {
    $rand = rand(1, 2);

    switch ($rand) {
      case 1:
        $this->size = 3;
        break;
      case 2:
        $this->size = 9;
        break;
    }

    $this->pictureName = "London Puzzle";
  }

  public
  function getSize(): int
  {
    return $this->size;
  }

  public
  function getPictureName(): string
  {
    return $this->pictureName;
  }
}
```

Now; let's put this all together in our `index.php` file:

```php
<?php

require_once('ToyFactory.php');
require_once('Toys/Toy.php');
require_once('Toys/MazeToy.php');
require_once('Toys/PuzzleToy.php');

require_once('SFToyFactory.php');
require_once('Toys/SFMazeToy.php');
require_once('Toys/SFPuzzleToy.php');

$sanFraciscoFactory = new SFToyFactory();
var_dump($sanFraciscoFactory->makeMaze());
echo "\n";
var_dump($sanFraciscoFactory->makePuzzle());
echo "\n";

require_once('UKToyFactory.php');
require_once('Toys/UKMazeToy.php');
require_once('Toys/UKPuzzleToy.php');

$britishToyFactory = new UKToyFactory();
var_dump($britishToyFactory->makeMaze());
echo "\n";
var_dump($britishToyFactory->makePuzzle());
echo "\n";
```

The output, if you run the given code, should look like the output shown in the following screenshot:

```
1   object(Toys\SFMazeToy)#2 (3) {
2     ["size":"Toys\SFMazeToy":private]=>
3     int(9)
4     ["pictureName":"Toys\SFMazeToy":private]=>
5     string(18) "San Francisco Maze"
6     ["type":"Toys\MazeToy":private]=>
7     string(4) "Maze"
8   }
9
10  object(Toys\SFPuzzleToy)#2 (3) {
11    ["size":"Toys\SFPuzzleToy":private]=>
12    int(3)
13    ["pictureName":"Toys\SFPuzzleToy":private]=>
14    string(20) "San Francisco Puzzle"
15    ["type":"Toys\PuzzleToy":private]=>
16    string(6) "Puzzle"
17  }
18
19  object(Toys\UKMazeToy)#3 (2) {
20    ["size":"Toys\UKMazeToy":private]=>
21    int(9)
22    ["pictureName":"Toys\UKMazeToy":private]=>
23    string(11) "London Maze"
24  }
25
26  object(Toys\UKPuzzleToy)#3 (3) {
27    ["size":"Toys\UKPuzzleToy":private]=>
28    int(9)
29    ["pictureName":"Toys\UKPuzzleToy":private]=>
30    string(13) "London Puzzle"
31    ["type":"Toys\PuzzleToy":private]=>
32    string(6) "Puzzle"
33  }
34
35
```

Now, suppose we want to add a new factory with a new set of products (for, say, New York), we simply add the toys `NYMazeToy` and the `NYPuzzleToy`, we could then create a new Factory called `NYToyFactory` (implementing the `ToyFactory` interface) and we would be done.

Now, the downsides of this class emerge when you need to add new product classes; the Abstract Factory needs updating, which violates the interface segregation principle. So it doesn't strictly meet the SOLID principles if you are going to need to add new product classes.

This design pattern can take some time to fully appreciate, so be sure to fiddle around with the source code and see what you can do with it.

Lazy initialization

Slappy Joe's burgers is a high quality restaurant where burgers are priced after they are made using the exact weight of the meat that was used. Unfortunately, due to the level of creation time, it would be a massive drain on resources for them to make every single type of burger before they are ordered.

Instead of having every type of burger ready for someone to order, when someone orders the burger, it is made (if it isn't already) and they are charged the price for it.

The `Burger.php` class is structured like this:

```php
<?php
class Burger
{
  private $cheese;
  private $chips;
  private $price;

  public function __construct(bool $cheese, bool $chips)
  {
    $this->cheese = $cheese;
    $this->chips = $chips;

    $this->price = rand(1, 2.50) + ($cheese ? 0.5 : 0) + ($chips ? 1 : 0);
  }

  public function getPrice(): int
  {
    return $this->price;
  }
}
```

Note that the price of the burger is only calculated after it is instantiated, meaning the customer can't be charged until it is made. The other function in the class simply returns the price of the burger.

Instead of instantiating from the `Burger` class directly, a lazy initialization class called `BurgerLazyLoader.php` is made, this class stores a list of instances of each burger that has been made; if a burger is requested that isn't made, it will make it. Alternatively, if a burger of a particular configuration already exists, that burger is returned.

Here is the `LazyLoader` class which instantiates `Burger` objects as needed:

```php
<?php
class BurgerLazyLoader
{
  private static $instances = array();

  public static function getBurger(bool $cheese, bool $chips): Burger
  {
    if (!isset(self::$instances[$cheese . $chips])) {
      self::$instances[$cheese . $chips] = new Burger($cheese, $chips);
    }

    return self::$instances[$cheese . $chips];
  }

  public static function getBurgerCount(): int
  {
    return count(self::$instances);
  }
}
```

The only other function added is the `getBurgerCount` function that returns a count of all the instances in the instances the `LazyLoader` has.

So let's wrap all of this together in our `index.php` file:

```php
<?php

require_once('Burger.php');
require_once('BurgerLazyLoader.php');

$burger = BurgerLazyLoader::getBurger(true, true);
echo "Burger with cheese and fries costs: £".$burger->getPrice();

echo "\n";
echo "Instances in lazy loader: ".BurgerLazyLoader::getBurgerCount();
echo "\n";

$burger = BurgerLazyLoader::getBurger(true, false);
echo "Burger with cheese and no fries costs: £".$burger->getPrice();

echo "\n";
echo "Instances in lazy loader: ".BurgerLazyLoader::getBurgerCount();
echo "\n";

$burger = BurgerLazyLoader::getBurger(true, true);
echo "Burger with cheese and fries costs: £".$burger->getPrice();
```

```
echo "\n";
echo "Instances in lazy loader: ".BurgerLazyLoader::getBurgerCount();
echo "\n";
```

We then get an output like this:

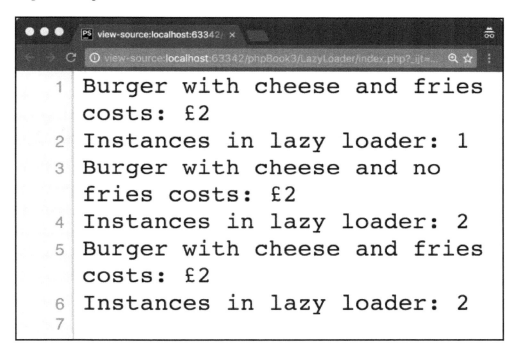

Given how the prices are random, you will notice the figures will be different, but the prices for the burger with cheese and fries remains the same the first and last time you call it. The instance is only created once; moreover, it is only created when it is needed, instead of being instantiated whenever it is wanted.

Hypothetical burger shop aside, this Creational pattern can have some great uses when you need it, such as when you need to delay the construction of an object from a class. This is often used when the constructor is an expensive or time-consuming operation.

If an object isn't already able to be used, one is created in a just-in-time fashion.

Builder pattern

When we reviewed the Factory design patterns, we saw how they were useful for enabling polymorphism. The crucial differentiation between Factory patterns and the Builder pattern is that the Builder pattern solely has the aim of resolving one anti-pattern and does not seek to perform polymorphism. The anti-pattern in question is the Telescoping Constructor.

The Telescoping Constructor problem is essentially where the count of arguments a constructor contains grows to an extent where it becomes impractical to use or even impractical to know which order the arguments go in.

Let's suppose we have a `Pizza` class as follows, it essentially contains a constructor and a `show` function which details the size and toppings of the pizza. The class looks like this:

```php
<?php

class Pizza
{

  private $size;
  private $cheese;
  private $pepperoni;
  private $bacon;

  public function __construct($size, $cheese, $pepperoni, $bacon)
  {
    $this->size = $size;
    $this->cheese = $cheese;
    $this->pepperoni = $pepperoni;
    $this->bacon = $bacon;
  }

  public function show()
  {
    $recipe = $this->size . " inch pizza with the following toppings: ";
    $recipe .= $this->cheese ? "cheese, " : "";
    $recipe .= $this->pepperoni ? "pepperoni, " : "";
    $recipe .= $this->bacon ? "bacon, " : "";

    return $recipe;
  }

}
```

Notice how many parameters the constructor contains, it literally contains the size and then every single topping. We can do better than this. In fact, let's aim to construct the pizza by adding all our parameters to a builder object that we can then use to create the pizza. This is what we're aiming for:

```php
$pizzaRecipe = (new PizzaBuilder(9))
  ->cheese(true)
  ->pepperoni(true)
  ->bacon(true)
  ->build();

$order = new Pizza($pizzaRecipe);
```

This isn't too hard to do; in fact you might even find it to be one of the easier design patterns we learn here. Let's first start by making a builder for our pizza, let's name this class `PizzaBuilder`:

```php
<?php

class PizzaBuilder
{
  public $size;
  public $cheese;
  public $pepperoni;
  public $bacon;

  public function __construct(int $size)
  {
    $this->size = $size;
  }

  public function cheese(bool $present): PizzaBuilder
  {
    $this->cheese = $present;
    return $this;
  }

  public function pepperoni(bool $present): PizzaBuilder
  {
    $this->pepperoni = $present;
    return $this;
  }

  public function bacon(bool $present): PizzaBuilder
  {
    $this->bacon = $present;
    return $this;
```

```
    }

    public function build()
    {
      return $this;
    }
  }
```

This class isn't too hard to understand, we have a constructor that sets the size, and for each additional topping we want to add we can then just call the relevant topping method with the parameter set to true or false accordingly. If the topping method isn't called, the topping in question isn't set as a parameter.

Finally, we have a build method, which can be called to run any last minute logic to organize data before it's sent into the constructor of the `Pizza` class. This said, I often don't like to do this, as this can be considered sequential coupling if methods need to be in a particular order and this would intrinsically defeat one purpose of us making a builder to do tasks like this.

For this reason, every topping method also returns the object that they are creating, allowing the output of any function to directly be injected into whatever class we want to use it to construct.

Next, let's adapt our `Pizza` class to utilize this builder:

```php
<?php

class Pizza
{

  private $size;
  private $cheese;
  private $pepperoni;
  private $bacon;

  public function __construct(PizzaBuilder $builder)
  {
    $this->size = $builder->size;
    $this->cheese = $builder->cheese;
    $this->pepperoni = $builder->pepperoni;
    $this->bacon = $builder->bacon;
  }

  public function show()
  {
    $recipe = $this->size . " inch pizza with the following toppings: ";
    $recipe .= $this->cheese ? "cheese, " : "";
```

```
$recipe .= $this->pepperoni ? "pepperoni, " : "";
$recipe .= $this->bacon ? "bacon, " : "";

return $recipe;
    }

}
```

It's quite straightforward for a constructor; we just access the `public` properties in the builder as and when they're needed.

Note that we can add additional validation of the data provided from the builder in the constructor here, though you can also add validation when you're setting the methods in the builder, depending on the type of logic required.

Now we can put all this together in our `index.php` file:

```php
<?php

require_once('Pizza.php');
require_once('PizzaBuilder.php');

$pizzaRecipe = (new PizzaBuilder(9))
  ->cheese(true)
  ->pepperoni(true)
  ->bacon(true)
  ->build();


$order = new Pizza($pizzaRecipe);
echo $order->show();
```

The output we should get looks something like this:

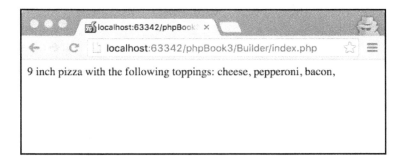

The Builder design pattern is incredibly easy to adopt but can save a lot of headaches when constructing objects.

The disadvantage of this method is the need for a separate Builder for every single class; this is the cost for such control over the object construction process.

Above this, the Builder design pattern allows you to vary the constructor variables and also provides for good encapsulation of the code that constructs an object itself. Like all design patterns, it's down to you to decide where it's most appropriate to use each one in your code.

Traditionally, key-value arrays were often used in substitution of Builder classes. Builder classes however, give you far more control over the construction process.

There's one other thing I should mention; here, we just referenced the methods using our `index.php` method; often, the methods we run there are placed in a class that can be referred to as the *Director* class.

Above this, you can also consider applying an interface to implement in your Builder if your Builder is going to have a lot of logic in.

Prototype pattern

The Prototype design pattern allows us to effectively duplicate objects while minimizing the performance impacts of having to re-instantiate an object.

You may have heard of prototypal languages if you've worked with JavaScript. In such languages, you work by cloning prototypal objects to create new objects; in turn, there is a reduced cost for creating new objects.

We have, so far, extensively discussed the use of the `__construct magic` method, but we haven't touched on the `__clone magic` method. The `__clone magic` method is what's run before an object is cloned (if possible); the method cannot be called directly and takes no parameters.

You might find it useful to use the `__clone` method when using this design pattern; that said, you might not need it depending on your use-case.

It's very important to remember that when we clone an object, the `__construct` function is not re-run. The object has already been constructed so PHP sees no reason to re-run it, so it's worth avoiding putting meaningful logic here when using this design pattern for this very reason.

Let's start off by defining a basic `Student` class:

```php
<?php

class Student
{
  public $name;
  public $year;
  public $grade;

  public function setName(string $name)
  {
    $this->name = $name;
  }

  public function setYear(int $year)
  {
    $this->year = $year;
  }

  public function setGrade(string $grade)
  {
    $this->grade = $grade;
  }

}
```

Now let's start building our `index.php` file, starting by including our `Student.php` class file:

```php
require_once('Student.php');
```

We can then create an instance of this class, set the various variables, and then `var_dump` the contents of the object so we can debug the details inside the object to see how it's working:

```php
$prototypeStudent = new Student();
$prototypeStudent->setName('Dave');
$prototypeStudent->setYear(2);
$prototypeStudent->setGrade('A*');

var_dump($prototypeStudent);
```

The output of this script looks like this:

```
object(Student)#1 (3) {
  ["name"]=>
  string(4) "Dave"
  ["year"]=>
  int(2)
  ["grade"]=>
  string(2) "A*"
}
```

So far, so good; we've essentially declared a basic class and set various properties. For our next challenge, let's clone this script. We can do this by adding the following lines to our `index.php` file:

```
$theLesserChild = clone $prototypeStudent;
$theLesserChild->setName('Mike');
$theLesserChild->setGrade('B');

var_dump($theLesserChild);
```

What does this look like? Well, take a look:

```
object(Student)#1 (3) {
  ["name"]=>
  string(4) "Dave"
  ["year"]=>
  int(2)
  ["grade"]=>
  string(2) "A*"
}
object(Student)#2 (3) {
  ["name"]=>
  string(4) "Mike"
  ["year"]=>
  int(2)
  ["grade"]=>
  string(1) "B"
}
```

So that seems straightforward enough; we've cloned an object and successfully changed the properties of that object. Our initial object, the prototype, has now been put into use by cloning it to build a new student.

And yes, we can do this again, as follows:

```
$theChildProdigy = clone $prototypeStudent;
$theChildProdigy->setName('Bob');
$theChildProdigy->setYear(3);
$theChildProdigy->setGrade('A');
```

But we can also do better; by using anonymous functions, otherwise known as closures, we can actually add extra methods dynamically to this object.

Let's define an anonymous function for our object:

```
$theChildProdigy->danceSkills = "Outstanding";
$theChildProdigy->dance = function (string $style) {
  return "Dancing $style style.";
};
```

Finally, let's echo out both a `var_dump` of the newly cloned object, but let's also execute the `dance` function we've just created:

```
var_dump($theChildProdigy);
var_dump($theChildProdigy->dance->__invoke('Pogo'));
```

You'll notice that in fact, we've had to use an __invoke magic method to call the anonymous function. This method is called when a script tries to call an object as a function; it is vital when calling anonymous functions in classes variables.

This is due to the fact that PHP class properties and methods are both in separate namespaces; in order to execute closures that are in class variables you either need to use __invoke; first, assign it to a class variable, use `call_user_func`, or use the __call magic method.

In this case, we just use the __invoke method.

Therefore, the output of the script looks like this:

```
object(Student)#1 (3) {
  ["name"]=>
  string(4) "Dave"
  ["year"]=>
  int(2)
  ["grade"]=>
  string(2) "A*"
}
object(Student)#2 (3) {
  ["name"]=>
  string(4) "Mike"
  ["year"]=>
  int(2)
  ["grade"]=>
  string(1) "B"
}
object(Student)#3 (5) {
  ["name"]=>
  string(3) "Bob"
  ["year"]=>
  int(3)
  ["grade"]=>
  string(1) "A"
  ["danceSkills"]=>
  string(11) "Outstanding"
  ["dance"]=>
  object(Closure)#4 (1) {
    ["parameter"]=>
    array(1) {
      ["$style"]=>
      string(10) "<required>"
    }
  }
}
string(19) "Dancing Pogo style."
```

Notice that our function ran at the very bottom?

The completed index.php file, therefore looks like this:

```php
<?php

require_once('Student.php');

$prototypeStudent = new Student();
$prototypeStudent->setName('Dave');
$prototypeStudent->setYear(2);
$prototypeStudent->setGrade('A*');

var_dump($prototypeStudent);

$theLesserChild = clone $prototypeStudent;
```

```
$theLesserChild->setName('Mike');
$theLesserChild->setGrade('B');

var_dump($theLesserChild);

$theChildProdigy = clone $prototypeStudent;
$theChildProdigy->setName('Bob');
$theChildProdigy->setYear(3);
$theChildProdigy->setGrade('A');

$theChildProdigy->danceSkills = "Outstanding";
$theChildProdigy->dance = function (string $style) {
  return "Dancing $style style.";
};

var_dump($theChildProdigy);
var_dump($theChildProdigy->dance->__invoke('Pogo'));
```

There are a few good use cases for this; suppose you want to perform transactions. You can take an object, clone it, and then replace the original if all the queries were successful and commit that cloned object to the database in place of the original.

It is a very useful and lightweight way to clone an object where you know that cloned object needs the same or nearly the same, contents as its parent object.

Summary

In this chapter, we started learning some critical PHP design patterns related to the creation of objects. We learned about various different Factory design patterns and how they can make your code more inline with common standards. We also covered how the Builder design pattern can help you avoid excessive arguments in your constructors. We also learned about lazy instantiation and how it can help your code be more efficient. Finally, we learned about how we can duplicate objects from prototype objects using the Prototype design pattern.

Continuing on with design patterns, in the next chapter we will talk about Structural design patterns.

4
Structural Design Patterns

Structural design patterns provide different ways to create class structure; for example, this can be how we use encapsulation to create bigger objects from smaller ones. They exist to ease the design by allowing us to identify simple ways to realize these relationships between entities.

In the last chapter, we covered how creational patterns can be used to determine how objects should be created; with structural patterns, we can determine the structure and relationship between classes.

After a brief note on Agile software architecture, in this chapter we will cover the following topics:

- Decorator pattern
- Class Adapter pattern
- Object Adapter pattern
- Flyweight pattern
- Composite pattern
- Bridge pattern
- Proxy pattern
- Facade pattern

Agile software architecture

Many organizations are leaning towards adopting an Agile form of project management. This bring about new concerns for the role of an architect; indeed, some view Agile and architecture to be in conflict. Two of the original signatories to the Agile manifesto, Martin Fowler and Robert Cecil Martin, have been vocally opposed to this idea. Indeed, Fowler is clear in clarifying the fact that while the Agile manifesto is hostile to large upfront design (such as the type you see in Prince2), Agile does not reject upfront design itself.

The computer scientist, Allen Holub, has a similar view. Agile focuses on doing things that are important for delivering software that is useful to the user, ahead of software that is merely useful for the salesman. In order for software to be of use in the long term it must be adaptable, extendable, and maintainable.

Fowler also has a vision for an architect within software development teams. Citing the fact that irreversible software is likely to give the most headaches later, this is where architectural decisions must lie. Above this, he claims that the role of an architect should be to seek to make these decisions reversible, thus mitigating the issue altogether.

During many large-scale software deployments, the phrase *we are at the point of no return* may be used. After the *point of no return*, it becomes unfeasible to revert the deployment to its original state. Software has its own *point of no return*, when it becomes the fact that software is harder to rewrite then it is to simply rebuild. While software may not reach the worst case of this *point of no return*, climbing up on the maintainability difficulty poses business difficulties.

Fowler also states that, in many cases, software architects do not even check that the software matches its original design. Through pair-programming with an architect, and indeed, the architect reviewing the code changes (that is, the pull requests), they can gain an understanding in order to provide feedback to the developer and also mitigate further technical debt.

In this book you may notice the lack of UML; that's because here I don't see UML as necessary. I mean, we are all speaking in PHP, right? You might find UML useful in your teams, though.

The process of architecture usually results in a deliverable; we call that deliverable an *artifact*. In Agile teams, those artifacts may be developed in an evolutionary way, rather than being an upfront product, but nevertheless it is perfectly possible to do architecture in an Agile setting.

Indeed, I would argue that architecture makes working in an Agile environment far easier. When programming to an interface or an abstract layer it is far easier to replace classes; in an Agile environment, requirements may change, meaning a class may need to be replaced. Software is only useful insofar as it is useful to the end client. Agile can help with this, but in order to be Agile, your code must be adaptive. Having great architecture is critical to this end.

When we write code, we should write code defensively. The adversary, however, isn't an enemy, it is ourselves. One of the quickest ways to degrade reliable code is by editing it to be weak.

Decorator

A Decorator is simply what adds additional functionality to an individual class without affecting the behavior of other objects from the same class.

The Single Responsibility Principle, simply put by Robert C. Martin (who I introduced at the start of this chapter), is that *a class should have only one reason to change*.

The principle states that every module or class should have a single responsibility and that responsibility should be entirely encapsulated by that class. All services of the class should align with that responsibility. Martin summarized this by defining the responsibility as follows:

> *"a charge assigned to a unique actor to signify its accountabilities concerning a unique business task".*

By using the Decorator design pattern, we are able to ensure that functionality is divided between classes with unique areas of concern, thus adhering to the Single Responsibility Principle.

Let's start off by declaring our Book interface. This is what we expect our Books to be able to produce:

```php
<?php

interface Book
{
    public function __construct(string $title, string $author, string
$contents);

    public function getTitle(): string;
```

```
   public function getAuthor(): string;

   public function getContents(): string;
}
```

Then we can declare our `EBook.php` class. This is the class we will be decorating with our `PrintBook` class:

```php
<?php

class EBook implements Book
{

  public $title;
  public $author;
  public $contents;

  public function __construct(string $title, string $author, string $contents)
  {
    $this->title = $title;
    $this->author = $author;
    $this->contents = $contents;
  }

  public function getTitle(): string
  {
    return $this->contents;
  }

  public function getAuthor(): string
  {
    return $this->author;
  }

  public function getContents(): string
  {
    return $this->contents;
  }
}
```

Now we can declare our `PrintBook` class. This is what we're using to decorate the `EBook` class:

```php
<?php

class PrintBook implements Book
{
```

```
    public $eBook;

    public function __construct(string $title, string $author, string
$contents)
    {
        $this->eBook = new EBook($title, $author, $contents);
    }

    public function getTitle(): string
    {
        return $this->eBook->getTitle();
    }

    public function getAuthor(): string
    {
        return $this->eBook->getAuthor();
    }

    public function getContents(): string
    {
        return $this->eBook->getContents();
    }

    public function getText(): string
    {
        $contents = $this->eBook->getTitle() . " by " .
$this->eBook->getAuthor();
        $contents .= "\n";
        $contents .= $this->eBook->getContents();

        return $contents;
    }
}
```

So now let's test all this with our `index.php` file:

```
<?php

require_once('Book.php');
require_once('EBook.php');
$PHPBook = new EBook("Mastering PHP Design Patterns", "Junade Ali", "Some
contents.");

require_once('PrintBook.php');
$PHPBook = new PrintBook("Mastering PHP Design Patterns", "Junade Ali",
"Some contents.");
echo $PHPBook->getText();
```

The output looks like this:

```
Some contents. by Junade Ali
Some contents.
```

Adapter

There are two types of Adapter pattern. I have a clear preference for Object Adapters over Class Adapters where possible; I will explain this in detail later.

The Adapter pattern allows an existing class to be used with an interface that it doesn't match. It is often used to allow existing classes to work with others without needing to alter their source code.

This can be quite useful in a polymorphic setting where you are using third-party libraries, each with their own interface.

Fundamentally, an Adapter helps two incompatible interfaces work together. Otherwise incompatible classes can be made to work together by converting the interface of one class into an interface expected by the clients.

Class Adapter

In a Class Adapter, we use inheritance to create an adapter. A class (the adapter) can inherit another (the adaptee); using standard inheritance we are able to add additional functionality to the adaptee.

Let's suppose we have an ATM class, in our ATM.php file:

```php
<?php

class ATM
{
  private $balance;

  public function __construct(float $balance)
  {
    $this->balance = $balance;
  }

  public function withdraw(float $amount): float
  {
    if ($this->reduceBalance($amount) === true) {
```

```php
      return $amount;
    } else {
      throw new Exception("Couldn't withdraw money.");
    }
  }

  protected function reduceBalance(float $amount): bool
  {
    if ($amount >= $this->balance) {
      return false;
    }

    $this->balance = ($this->balance - $amount);
    return true;
  }

  public function getBalance(): float
  {
    return $this->balance;
  }
}
```

Let's create our `ATMWithPhoneTopUp.php` to form our adapter:

```php
<?php

class ATMWithPhoneTopUp extends ATM
{
  public function getTopUp(float $amount, int $time): string
  {
    if ($this->reduceBalance($amount) === true) {
      return $this->generateTopUpCode($amount, $time);
    } else {
      throw new Exception("Couldn't withdraw money.");
    }
  }

  private function generateTopUpCode(float $amount, int $time): string
  {
    return $amount . $time . rand(0, 10000);
  }
}
```

Let's wrap this all together in an `index.php` file:

```php
<?php

require_once('ATM.php');
```

```
$atm = new ATM(500.00);
$atm->withdraw(50);
echo $atm->getBalance();
echo "\n";

require_once('ATMWithPhoneTopUp.php');

$adaptedATM = new ATMWithPhoneTopUp(500.00);
echo "Top-up code: " . $adaptedATM->getTopUp(50, time());
echo "\n";
echo $adaptedATM->getBalance();
```

Now that we have adapted our initial ATM class to yield top-up codes, we can now utilize this new top-up functionality. The output of all this is as follows:

```
450
Top-up code: 5014606939121598
450
```

Note that if we wanted to adapt to multiple adaptees, this would be difficult in PHP.

In PHP, multiple inheritance isn't possible, unless you are working with Traits. In this case, we can only adapt one class to match the interface of another.

The other key architectural reason for us not using this approach is that it is often good design to prefer composition over inheritance (as described by the Composite Reuse Principle).

In order to explore this principle in more detail, we need to take a look at Object Adapters.

Object Adapter

The Composite Reuse Principle states that classes should achieve polymorphic behavior and code reuse by their composition.

By applying this principle, classes should contain instances of other classes when they want to implement a particular piece of functionality, as opposed to inheriting the functionality from a base or parent class.

For this reason, the Gang of Four stated the following:

"Favor 'object composition' over 'class inheritance'."

Why is this principle so vital? Consider our last example, where we used class inheritance; in such a case, there is no formal guarantee that our adapter would match the interface we want it to. What if the parent class exposed a function we didn't want the adapter to? Composition gives us more control.

By using composition over inheritance, we are able to better support the polymorphic behavior that is so vital in object-oriented programming.

Let's suppose we have a class to generate an insurance premium. It provides a monthly premium and an annual premium depending on how the customer wants to pay their premium. By paying annually, the customer gets a saving equivalent to half a month:

```php
<?php

class Insurance
{
  private $limit;
  private $excess;

  public function __construct(float $limit, float $excess)
  {
    if ($excess >= $limit) {
      throw New Exception('Excess must be less than premium.');
    }

    $this->limit = $limit;
    $this->excess = $excess;
  }

  public function monthlyPremium(): float
  {
    return ($this->limit-$this->excess)/200;
  }

  public function annualPremium(): float
  {
    return $this->monthlyPremium()*11.5;
  }
}
```

Let's suppose a market comparison tool polymorphically uses classes such as the one mentioned earlier to actually go ahead and calculate insurance quotes from multiple different vendors; they use this interface to do this:

```php
<?php

interface MarketCompare
```

```php
{
  public function __construct(float $limit, float $excess);
  public function getAnnualPremium();
  public function getMonthlyPremium();
}
```

Accordingly, we can use this interface to build an Object Adapter to ensure our `Insurance` class, our premium generator, matches the interface that the market comparison tool is expecting:

```php
<?php

class InsuranceMarketCompare implements MarketCompare
{
  private $premium;

  public function __construct(float $limit, float $excess)
  {
    $this->premium = new Insurance($limit, $excess);
  }

  public function getAnnualPremium(): float
  {
    return $this->premium->annualPremium();
  }

  public function getMonthlyPremium(): float
  {
    return $this->premium->monthlyPremium();
  }
}
```

Note how the class actually goes ahead and instantiates its own class for what it's trying to adapt.

The adapter then stores this class in a `private` variable. We then use this object in the `private` variable to proxy requests.

An Adapter, both a Class Adapter and an Object Adapter, should act as glue code. What I mean by that is that adapters shouldn't perform any calculations or computation, they merely act as a proxy between incompatible interfaces.

It is standard practice to keep logic out of our glue code and leave the logic down to the code that we are adapting. If, in doing this, we come up against the Single Responsibility Principle, we need to adapt another class.

As I mentioned earlier, adapting multiple classes isn't really possible in a Class Adapter, so you'd either have to wrap such logic in a Trait or we would need to use an Object Adapter, such as the one we're discussing here.

Let's try out this adapter. We'll do so by writing the following `index.php` file to see if our new class matches the expected interface:

```php
<?php

require_once('Insurance.php');

$quote = new Insurance(10000, 250);
echo $quote->monthlyPremium();
echo "\n";

require_once('MarketCompare.php');
require_once('InsuranceMarketCompare.php');

$quote = new InsuranceMarketCompare(10000, 250);
echo $quote->getMonthlyPremium();
echo "\n";
echo $quote->getAnnualPremium();
```

The output should look something like this:

```
48.75
48.75
560.625
```

The key drawback of this method, compared to the Class Adapter method, is that we must implement common methods, even if those methods are merely forwarding methods.

FlyWeight

Like in real life, not all objects are easy to create, and some can take up excessive amounts of memory. The FlyWeight design pattern can help us minimize memory usage by sharing as much data as possible with similar objects.

This design pattern has limited use in most PHP applications, but it is still worth knowing it for the odd situation where it is incredibly useful.

Suppose we have a `Shape` interface with a `draw` method:

```php
<?php

interface Shape
{
  public function draw();
}
```

Let's create a `Circle` class that implements this interface. When implementing this, we build the ability to set the location of a circle with X and Y co-ordinates. We also create the ability to set the circle's radius and draw it (print out this information). Note how the color characteristic is set outside the class.

There's a very important reason for this. In our example, the color is state-independent; it is an intrinsic part of the circle. The location and size of the circle are, however, state-dependent and are therefore extrinsic. The extrinsic state information is passed to the FlyWeight object when its functions are needed; the intrinsic options, however, are independent of each process of the FlyWeight. This will make more sense when we cover how this factory is made.

This is the important information:

- **Extrinsic**: State belongs to the external context of the object and is input into the object when it's used.
- **Intrinsic**: State that naturally belongs to the object and therefore should be permanent, immutable (internal), or context-free.

With this in mind, let's put together an implementation of our `Shape` interface. Here's our `Circle` class:

```php
<?php

class Circle implements Shape
{

  private $colour;
  private $x;
  private $y;
  private $radius;

  public function __construct(string $colour)
  {
    $this->colour = $colour;
  }
```

```php
public function setX(int $x)
{
  $this->x = $x;
}

public function setY(int $y)
{
  $this->y = $y;
}

public function setRadius(int $radius)
{
  $this->radius = $radius;
}

public function draw()
{
  echo "Drawing circle which is " . $this->colour . " at [" . $this->x .
", " . $this->y . "] of radius " . $this->radius . ".";
  echo "\n";
}
}
```

With this, we can now build our `ShapeFactory`, which actually implements the FlyWeight pattern. An object with the color of our choice is instantiated when it's needed, and is then stored for later use:

```php
<?php

class ShapeFactory
{
  private $shapeMap = array();

  public function getCircle(string $colour)
  {
    $circle = 'Circle' . '_' . $colour;

    if (!isset($this->shapeMap[$circle])) {
      echo "Creating a ".$colour." circle.";
      echo "\n";
      $this->shapeMap[$circle] = new Circle($colour);
    }

    return $this->shapeMap[$circle];
  }
}
```

Let's demonstrate how this works in our `index.php` file.

In order for this to work, we create 100 objects with random colors, in a random location:

```php
require_once('Shape.php');
require_once('Circle.php');
require_once('ShapeFactory.php');

$colours = array('red', 'blue', 'green', 'black', 'white', 'orange');

$factory = new ShapeFactory();

for ($i = 0; $i < 100; $i++) {
  $randomColour = $colours[array_rand($colours)];

  $circle = $factory->getCircle($randomColour);
  $circle->setX(rand(0, 100));
  $circle->setY(rand(0, 100));
  $circle->setRadius(100);

  $circle->draw();
}
```

Now, let's take a look at the output. You can see we've drawn 100 circles, but we have only needed to instantiate a handful of circles as we are caching objects of the same color for later use:

```
Creating a green circle.
Drawing circle which is green at [29, 26] of radius 100.
Creating a black circle.
Drawing circle which is black at [17, 64] of radius 100.
Drawing circle which is black at [81, 86] of radius 100.
Drawing circle which is black at [0, 73] of radius 100.
Creating a red circle.
Drawing circle which is red at [10, 15] of radius 100.
Drawing circle which is red at [70, 79] of radius 100.
Drawing circle which is red at [13, 78] of radius 100.
Drawing circle which is green at [78, 27] of radius 100.
Creating a blue circle.
Drawing circle which is blue at [38, 11] of radius 100.
Creating a orange circle.
Drawing circle which is orange at [43, 57] of radius 100.
Drawing circle which is blue at [58, 65] of radius 100.
Drawing circle which is orange at [75, 67] of radius 100.
Drawing circle which is green at [92, 59] of radius 100.
Drawing circle which is blue at [53, 3] of radius 100.
Drawing circle which is black at [14, 33] of radius 100.
Creating a white circle.
Drawing circle which is white at [84, 46] of radius 100.
Drawing circle which is green at [49, 61] of radius 100.
```

```
Drawing circle which is orange at [57, 44] of radius 100.
Drawing circle which is orange at [64, 33] of radius 100.
Drawing circle which is white at [42, 74] of radius 100.
Drawing circle which is green at [5, 91] of radius 100.
Drawing circle which is white at [87, 36] of radius 100.
Drawing circle which is red at [74, 94] of radius 100.
Drawing circle which is black at [19, 6] of radius 100.
Drawing circle which is orange at [70, 83] of radius 100.
Drawing circle which is green at [74, 64] of radius 100.
Drawing circle which is white at [89, 21] of radius 100.
Drawing circle which is red at [25, 23] of radius 100.
Drawing circle which is blue at [68, 96] of radius 100.
Drawing circle which is green at [74, 6] of radius 100.
```

You may have noticed something here. The way I'm storing the cache of the FlyWeight object that we are reusing is by concatenating the *Circle_* and the color, for example *Circle_green*. Obviously, this works in this use case, but there is a better way of doing this; in PHP, it is actually possible to get a unique ID for a given object. We'll cover this in the next pattern.

Composite

Imagine an audio system consisting of individual songs and also playlists of songs. Yes, playlists consist of songs, but we want both to be treated individually. Both are types of music, both can be played.

The Composite design pattern can help here; it allows us to ignore the differences between compositions of objects and individual objects. It allows us to treat both with identical or nearly-identical code.

Let's put together a little example; a song is our example of a *leaf*, with playlists being *composites*. Music is our abstraction of playlists and songs; therefore, we can call this our *component*. The *client* of all this is our index.php file.

By not discriminating between leaf-nodes and branches, our code becomes less complex and therefore less error prone.

Let's start by defining an interface for our Music:

```php
<?php

interface Music
{
  public function play();
```

```
      }
```

Now let's put together some implementations, starting with our Song class:

```php
<?php

class Song implements Music
{
  public $id;
  public $name;

  public function   __construct(string $name)
  {
    $this->id = uniqid();
    $this->name = $name;
  }

  public function play()
  {
    printf("Playing song #%s, %s.\n", $this->id, $this->name);
  }
}
```

Now we can start to put together our Playlist class. In this example, you may notice I set the key in the songs array using a function called spl_object_hash. This function is an absolutely blessing when dealing with arrays of objects.

What this function does is return a unique hash for each object which remains consistent so long as the object is not destroyed, regardless of what properties of the class are changed. It provides a stable way of addressing arbitrary objects. Once the object is destroyed, the hash can then be reused for other objects.

The contents of the object are not hashed by this function; it merely acts to show the internal handle and the hander table pointer. This means that if you alter the properties of an object, the hash will not change. This said, it does not guarantee uniqueness. If an object is destroyed and one of the same class is immediately created afterwards you will get the same hash as PHP will reuse the same internal handle after the first class has been dereferenced and destroyed.

This will be true, as PHP can use the internal handle:

```php
var_dump(spl_object_hash(new stdClass()) === spl_object_hash(new
stdClass()));
```

However, this will be false, as PHP must create a new handler:

```php
$object = new StdClass();
var_dump(spl_object_hash($object) === spl_object_hash(new stdClass()));
```

Now let's return to our `Playlist` class. Let's implement our `Music` interface with it; so, here's the class:

```php
<?php

class Playlist implements Music
{
  private $songs = array();

  public function addSong(Music $content): bool
  {
    $this->songs[spl_object_hash($content)] = $content;
    return true;
  }

  public function removeItem(Music $content): bool
  {
    unset($this->songs[spl_object_hash($content)]);
    return true;
  }

  public function play()
  {
    foreach ($this->songs as $content) {
      $content->play();
    }
  }
}
```

Now let's put this all together in our `index.php` file. What we're doing here is creating some song objects, some of which we will assign to a playlist using their `addSong` function.

Because playlists are implemented in the same way as songs, we can even use the `addSong` function with other playlists (in this case, it may be better for us to rename the `addSong` function `addMusic`).

Then we play the parent playlist. This plays the child playlists and in turn plays all the songs in those playlists as well:

```php
<?php

require_once('Music.php');
```

```
require_once('Playlist.php');
require_once('Song.php');

$songOne = new Song('Lost In Stereo');
$songTwo = new Song('Running From Lions');
$songThree = new Song('Guts');
$playlistOne = new Playlist();
$playlistTwo = new Playlist();
$playlistThree = new Playlist();
$playlistTwo->addSong($songOne);
$playlistTwo->addSong($songTwo);
$playlistThree->addSong($songThree);
$playlistOne->addSong($playlistTwo);
$playlistOne->addSong($playlistThree);
$playlistOne->play();
```

When we run this script, we can see the expected output:

```
Playing song #57106d5adb364, Lost In Stereo.
Playing song #57106d5adb63a, Running From Lions.
Playing song #57106d5adb654, Guts.
```

Bridge

The Bridge pattern can be quite straightforward; it effectively allows us to decouple an abstraction from an implementation so the two can vary independently.

When classes vary frequently, bridging an interface and a concrete class allows developers to vary their classes with greater ease.

Let's propose a generic messenger interface that has the ability to send some form of message, Messenger.php:

```php
<?php

interface Messenger
{
  public function send($body);
}
```

One specific implementation of this interface is an InstantMessenger application, InstantMessenger.php:

```php
<?php

class InstantMessenger implements Messenger
```

```
{
  public function send($body)
  {
    echo "InstantMessenger: " . $body;
  }
}
```

Similarly, we can do the same with an SMS application, SMS.php:

```
<?php

class SMS implements Messenger
{
  public function send($body)
  {
    echo "SMS: " . $body;
  }
}
```

We can now create an interface for the physical device, the transmitter, if you will,
Transmitter.php:

```
<?php

interface Transmitter
{
  public function setSender(Messenger $sender);

  public function send($body);
}
```

We can decouple a transmitter from the devices that implement its methods by using a
Device class. The Device class bridges the Transmitter interface to the physical device,
Device.php:

```
<?php

abstract class Device implements Transmitter
{
  protected $sender;

  public function setSender(Messenger $sender)
  {
    $this->sender = $sender;
  }
}
```

So let's put together a concrete class to represent a phone, `Phone.php`:

```php
<?php

class Phone extends Device
{
  public function send($body)
  {
    $body .= "\n\n Sent from a phone.";

    return $this->sender->send($body);
  }
}
```

And let's do the same for a `Tablet`. `Tablet.php` is:

```php
<?php

class Tablet extends Device
{
  public function send($body)
  {
    $body .= "\n\n Sent from a Tablet.";

    return $this->sender->send($body);
  }
}
```

Finally, let's wrap this all together in an `index.php` file:

```php
<?php

require_once('Transmitter.php');
require_once('Device.php');
require_once('Phone.php');
require_once('Tablet.php');

require_once('Messenger.php');
require_once('SMS.php');
require_once('InstantMessenger.php');

$phone = new Phone();
$phone->setSender(new SMS());

$phone->send("Hello there!");
```

The output of this is as follows:

```
SMS: Hello there!

 Sent from a phone.
```

Proxy pattern

Proxy is a class that is merely an interface to something else. It may be an interface to anything; from being a network connection, a file, a large object in memory, or any other resource that is too difficult to duplicate.

In our example here, we will simply be creating a simple proxy to forward to one of two objects depending on how the proxy is instantiated.

Accessing a simple Proxy class allows the client to access both feeders for cats and dogs from one object, depending on whether it's been instantiated.

Let's start off by defining an interface for our `AnimalFeeder`:

```php
<?php

namespace IcyApril\PetShop;

interface AnimalFeeder
{
  public function __construct(string $petName);

  public function dropFood(int $hungerLevel, bool $water = false): string;

  public function displayFood(int $hungerLevel): string;
}
```

We can then define two animal feeders for a cat and a dog:

```php
<?php

namespace IcyApril\PetShop\AnimalFeeders;


use IcyApril\PetShop\AnimalFeeder;

class Cat implements AnimalFeeder
{
  public function __construct(string $petName)
  {
```

```php
    $this->petName = $petName;
  }

  public function dropFood(int $hungerLevel, bool $water = false): string
  {
    return $this->selectFood($hungerLevel) . ($water ? ' with water' : '');
  }

  public function displayFood(int $hungerLevel): string
  {
    return $this->selectFood($hungerLevel);
  }

  protected function selectFood(int $hungerLevel): string
  {
    switch ($hungerLevel) {
      case 0:
        return 'lamb';
        break;
      case 1:
        return 'chicken';
        break;
      case 3:
        return 'tuna';
        break;
    }
  }
}
```

And here's our dog `AnimalFeeder`:

```php
<?php

namespace IcyApril\PetShop\AnimalFeeders;

class Dog
{
  public function __construct(string $petName)
  {
    if (strlen($petName) > 10) {
      throw new \Exception('Name too long.');
    }

    $this->petName = $petName;
  }
```

```php
  public function dropFood(int $hungerLevel, bool $water = false): string
  {
    return $this->selectFood($hungerLevel) . ($water ? ' with water' : '');
  }

  public function displayFood(int $hungerLevel): string
  {
    return $this->selectFood($hungerLevel);
  }

  protected function selectFood(int $hungerLevel): string
  {
    if ($hungerLevel == 3) {
      return "chicken and vegetables";
    } elseif (date('H') < 10) {
      return "turkey and beef";
    } else {
      return "chicken and rice";
    }
  }
}
```

With this defined, we can now make our proxy class, a class that essentially uses the constructor to decipher what kind of class it needs to instantiate, then redirects all function calls to this class. In order to redirect function calls, the __call magic method is used.

This looks something like this:

```php
<?php

namespace IcyApril\PetShop;

class AnimalFeederProxy
{
  protected $instance;

  public function __construct(string $feeder, string $name)
  {
    $class = __NAMESPACE__ . '\\AnimalFeeders' . $feeder;
    $this->instance = new $class($name);
  }

  public function __call($name, $arguments)
  {
    return call_user_func_array([$this->instance, $name], $arguments);
  }
}
```

You might have noticed that we have to manually create the class in the constructor with the namespace. We do this using the __NAMESPACE__ `magic` constant to find the current namespace, then concatenating it onto the specific sub-namespace where the classes are. Note that we have to escape the \ using another \ in order to allow us to specify the namespace without PHP interpreting \ as an escape character.

Let's build our `index.php` file and utilize the proxy class to build objects:

```php
<?php

require_once('AnimalFeeder.php');
require_once('AnimalFeederProxy.php');


require_once('AnimalFeeders/Cat.php');
$felix = new \IcyApril\PetShop\AnimalFeederProxy('Cat', 'Felix');
echo $felix->displayFood(1);
echo "\n";
echo $felix->dropFood(1, true);
echo "\n";

require_once('AnimalFeeders/Dog.php');
$brian = new \IcyApril\PetShop\AnimalFeederProxy('Dog', 'Brian');
echo $brian->displayFood(1);
echo "\n";
echo $brian->dropFood(1, true);
```

The output is as follows:

```
chicken
chicken with water
turkey and beef
turkey and beef with water
```

So how can you use this in reality? Suppose you got a record out of the database that contained an object that detailed the animal type and name; you could just pass this object to the constructor of the Proxy class and use that as a mechanism to create your classes.

In practice, this has a great use case when it comes to supporting resource-hungry objects that you don't necessarily want to instantiate unless they are really required by the client; the same can be true of resource-hungry network connections and other types of resource.

Facade

Facade (also known as *Façade*) design patterns are a curious thing; they essentially act as a simple interface to a complex system. A Facade design pattern works providing a single class that in itself instantiates other classes and provides a simple interface to use those functions.

A warning when using such pattern is that, as classes are instantiated within the Facade, you are essentially tightly coupling the classes that it utilizes. There are cases where you want this, but there are cases where you do not. Where do you do not want this behavior, you are better suited to using dependency injection.

I have found this to be useful when wrapping a set of poor APIs into a single unified API. It reduces external dependencies, allowing complexity to be internalized; this process can make your code more readable.

I shall demonstrate this pattern in a crude example, but this will effectively make the mechanism obvious.

Let me propose three classes for a toy factory.

Manufacturer (the factory building the toy) is a simple class that is instantiated with the capacity of how many toys to build at a time:

```php
<?php

class Manufacturer
{
  private $capacity;

  public function __construct(int $capacity)
  {
    $this->capacity = $capacity;
  }

  public function build(): string
  {
    return uniqid();
  }
}
```

Post class (the shipping courier) is a simple function that dispatches the toy from the factory:

```php
<?php

class Post
{
  private $sender;

  public function __construct(string $sender)
  {
    $this->sender = $sender;
  }

  public function dispatch(string $item, string $to): bool
  {
    if (strlen($item) !== 13) {
      return false;
    }

    if (empty($to)) {
      return false;
    }

    return true;
  }
}
```

An SMS class informs the client that their toy has been dispatched from the factory:

```php
<?php

class SMS
{
  private $from;

  public function __construct(string $from)
  {
    $this->from = $from;
  }

  public function send(string $to, string $message): bool
  {
    if (empty($to)) {
      return false;
    }

    if (strlen($message) === 0) {
```

```
      return false;
   }

   echo $to . " received message: " . $message;
   return true;
  }
}
```

Here is our `ToyFactory` class, which acts as a Facade to link together all these classes and allow operations to happen sequentially:

```php
<?php

class ToyShop
{
  private $courier;
  private $manufacturer;
  private $sms;

  public function __construct(String $factoryAdress, String $contactNumber,
int $capacity)
  {
    $this->courier = new Post($factoryAdress);
    $this->sms = new SMS($contactNumber);
    $this->manufacturer = new Manufacturer($capacity);
  }

  public function processOrder(string $address, $phone)
  {
    $item = $this->manufacturer->build();
    $this->courier->dispatch($item, $address);
    $this->sms->send($phone, "Your order has been shipped.");
  }
}
```

And finally, we can wrap all this together in our `index.php` file:

```php
<?php

require_once('Manufacturer.php');
require_once('Post.php');
require_once('SMS.php');
require_once('ToyShop.php');

$childrensToyFactory = new ToyShop('1 Factory Lane, Oxfordshire',
'07999999999', 5);
$childrensToyFactory->processOrder('8 Midsummer Boulevard', '07123456789');
```

Once we run this code, we see the message from our SMS class showing the text message was sent:

In other situations, where the various classes were loosely coupled together, we may find it better to use dependency injection. By injecting objects that perform various actions into the ToyFactory class we can benefit from making testing easier by being able to inject fake classes that the ToyFactory class can manipulate.

Personally, I am a huge believer in making code as easily testable as possible; hence why I don't like this approach.

Summary

This chapter extended the design patterns we started to learn in the previous chapter by introducing structural design patterns.

To this end, we learned some critical patterns to ease the software design process; these patterns identify a simple way to realize the relationships between different entities:

- We learned about the Decorator, how to wrap classes to add additional behavior to them, and critically, we learned how this can help us comply with the Single Responsibility Principle.
- We learned about Class and Object Adapters, and the difference between them. The critical takeaway here is the arguments for why we may choose composition over inheritance.
- We reviewed the FlyWeight design pattern, which can help us perform certain processes in a memory-efficient manner.
- We learned how the Composite design pattern can help us treat compositions of objects the same as individual objects.

- We covered the Bridge design pattern, which lets us decouple our abstraction from its implementation, allowing the two to vary independently.
- We covered how the Proxy design pattern can function as an interface to another class and how we can use this as a forwarding agent.
- Finally, we learned how the Facade design pattern can be used to provide a simple interface to a complex system.

In the next chapter, we will wrap up our design patterns section by talking about Behavioral patterns, ready to touch on Architectural patterns.

5
Behavioral Design Patterns

Behavioral design patterns are all about the communication between objects.

Bearing in mind the Single Responsibility Principle, it is vital that classes only encapsulate one responsibility. Given this, there is clearly a necessity to allow objects to communicate.

By using Behavioral design patterns, we are able to increase the flexibility by which we conduct these communications.

In this chapter, we'll cover the following patterns:

- Observer pattern (SplObserver/SplSubject)
- Iterator
- The many Iterators of PHP
- Generators
- Template pattern
- Chain of Responsibility pattern
- Strategy pattern
- Specification pattern
- Scheduled Task pattern

Personality traits for passionate programmers

Before we start talking about Behavioral design patterns, let's talk about your behavior as a developer. Earlier in this book I've talked about how often development failures emerge as a result of bad management practices.

Let's imagine two scenarios:

- A company introduces Scrum as a methodology (or another *Agile* methodology that is lacking in technical knowledge), without their code being agile enough to withstand code. In these scenarios, when a code is added, it is often botched into place and it will almost certainly be the case that the code takes far longer to implement than it would without technical debt. This leads to a slow development speed.
- Alternatively, a company follows a strictly pre-defined process and that methodology is set in stone. These processes are often unjustifiable but developers often follow them as they aren't educated in better processes, don't want to enter a bureaucratic dispute to alter them, or may even fear disciplinary action for attempting to improve a process.

In both these scenarios, a poor process is at the heart of the problem. Even when you're not dealing with a legacy project, this can become a problem due to the change of requirements throughout a property. A good property of software is the ability to change and, indeed, change the design of the software itself (we'll discuss this in the final chapter on refactoring).

Alastair Cockburn identified that software developers don't often fit into a pre-defined production-line process. Humans are unpredictable, and when they are the key actor in any given process, the process also becomes unpredictable. Humans are open to error and don't act perfectly in a pre-defined process when there is as much room for error as there is in software development. Fundamentally, this is why people must come before processes, as stated in the Agile manifesto. The developers must come before the process.

Some of those in management positions want to buy something called Agile. They'll hire a consultant who fails to understand how software development can really be made a success, and instead, implements a ridiculous process as part of a cash cow operation to sell Agile. I believe that Scrum is the worst example of this (in part because of the number of inaccurate courses and pseudo-qualifications), but no doubt other Agile processes can be used as cash cows.

I have repeatedly come into contact with managers or **Scrum Masters** who claim that *Scrum says we should do ...* or *Agile says we should do ....* This is mentally illogical and should be avoided. When you make this statement you are fundamentally not understanding that an Agile methodology is based on the principle of agility, and as such, people must come above processes.

Let's review the first scenario again. Note that the dispute largely emerges from a lack of development quality instead of project management processes. Scrum fails to implement development processes and as a result, projects attempted through Scrum may often fail.

Extreme Programming (XP) contains these development rules, which Scrum lacks. Here are some examples:

- Coding standards (in PHP, you may choose the PSR standards we discussed in earlier chapters)
- Write the unit test first and the code should be written so it passes the test
- All production code is pair-programmed
- A dedicated integration server with only one pair integration code at a time with code being integrated frequently
- Use collective ownership; no part of the codebase is off limits to another developer

This is all completed against a backdrop of fixing XP when it breaks, making improving the process a regular part of development.

Introducing technical standards and development rules requires both a pre-existing knowledge of development with a passion for learning more; for this, a logical and evidence-driven thought process is vital. These are all critical elements of being a great software engineer.

Pair-programming must not become an effort in mentoring, it mustn't be a student-teacher relationship; both developers must be willing to put forward ideas and have such ideas criticized. Indeed, it is vital to be able to learn from each other.

In an Agile relationship, everyone must be willing to understand and contribute to the planning process, as such communication is a vital skill. Similarly, respect for each other is key; everyone from customers to developers deserves respect. Developers must be courageous in many ways, not least being truthful about progress and estimation while crucially also adapting to change. We must seek to understand the feedback we receive before addressing or dismissing it.

These skills aren't merely toggles or switches, they are open-ended skills and knowledge bases that we must seek to maintain and exercise. Things go wrong; through the use of feedback, we are able to ensure our code is of a sufficiently high quality before it is deployed.

Observer pattern (SplObserver/SplSubject)

The Observer design pattern essentially allows an object (the subject) to maintain a list of observers that are automatically notified when the state of the that object changes.

This pattern applies a one-to-many dependency between objects; there is always one subject that updates many observers.

The Gang of Four originally identified that this pattern was particularly applicable in cases where an abstraction has two aspects, with one dependent on the other. In addition to this, it is very useful when a change to object requires changes to the others and you don't know how many other objects need to be changed. Finally, this pattern is also incredibly useful when an object should notify other objects without making assumptions about what those objects are, thus making this pattern great for loosely coupling this relationship.

PHP provides a very useful interface called `SplObserver` and `SplSubject`. These interfaces provide the template for implementing the Observer design pattern while not actually implementing any functionality.

In essence, when we implement this pattern we allow an unlimited amount of objects to observe events in the subjects.

By calling an `attach` method in the `subject` object, we can attach an observer to the subject. When a change occurs in the subject, the subject's `notify` method can iterate through the observers and call their `update` method polymorphically.

We are also able to call an un-notify method in the subject which will allow us to stop an `observer` object from observing a `subject` object.

Given this, the `Subject` class contains methods to attach and detach observers from itself, the class also contains a `notify` method to update the observers that are looking at it. Therefore, PHP's `SplSubject` interface is as follows:

```
interface SplSubject {
  public function attach (SplObserver $observer);
  public function detach (SplObserver $observer);
  public function notify ();
```

```
}
```

Compared to this, our SplObserver interface looks even more simple; it merely needs to implement a single method that allows the subjects to update the observers:

```
interface SplObserver {
  public function update (SplSubject $subject);
}
```

Now, let's see how we can implement these two interfaces to implement this design pattern. In this example, we will have a news feed class that will update various readers that are reading the classes.

Let's define our Feed class, which will implement the SplSubject interface:

```php
<?php

class Feed implements SplSubject
{
  private $name;
  private $observers = array();
  private $content;

  public function __construct($name)
  {
    $this->name = $name;
  }

  public function attach(SplObserver $observer)
  {
    $observerHash = spl_object_hash($observer);
    $this->observers[$observerHash] = $observer;
  }

  public function detach(SplObserver $observer)
  {
    $observerHash = spl_object_hash($observer);
    unset($this->observers[$observerHash]);
  }

  public function breakOutNews($content)
  {
    $this->content = $content;
    $this->notify();
  }

  public function getContent()
  {
```

```
      return $this->content . " on ". $this->name . ".";
  }

  public function notify()
  {
    foreach ($this->observers as $value) {
      $value->update($this);
    }
  }
}
```

The implementation we covered is, overall, quite simple. Notice how it's using the spl_object_hash function that we explored previously in this book to allow us to easily detach objects. By using the hash as the key for the array we are able to rapidly find a given object without needing to do it.

Now we can define our Reader class, which will implement the SplObserver interface:

```php
<?php

class Reader implements SplObserver
{
  private $name;

  public function __construct($name)
  {
    $this->name = $name;
  }

  public function update(SplSubject $subject)
  {
    echo $this->name . ' is reading the article ' . $subject->getContent()
. ' ';
  }
}
```

Let's wrap all this together in our index.php file as follows:

```php
<?php

require_once('Feed.php');
require_once('Reader.php');

$newspaper = new  Feed('Junade.com');

$allen = new Reader('Mark');
$jim = new Reader('Lily');
$linda = new Reader('Caitlin');
```

```
//add reader
$newspaper->attach($allen);
$newspaper->attach($jim);
$newspaper->attach($linda);

//remove reader
$newspaper->detach($linda);

//set break outs
$newspaper->breakOutNews('PHP Design Patterns');
```

In this script, we firstly instantiate a feed with three readers. We attach all of them, then detach one. Finally, we send a new alert, which produces the following output:

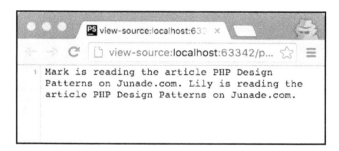

The main advantage of this design pattern surrounds the loosely coupled nature of the relationships between the observers and the subjects. There is greater modularity, as subjects and observers can independently vary. In addition to this, we can add as many observers as we want, providing as many pieces of functionality as we're after. This extensibility and customization is often the reason this design pattern is applied in the context of view for an application and is also often implemented in **Model-View-Controller (MVC)** frameworks.

The disadvantages of using this pattern come when we need to debug this whole thing; flow control can become difficult as observers don't know about each other. In addition to this, there is an update overhead, which can make memory management difficult when dealing with particularly large observers.

Remember that this design pattern is solely for use within one program, it's not designed for inter-process communication or a messaging system. Later in this book, we'll cover how you can use Messaging patterns to describe how different parts of a message parsing system interconnect when we want to allow intercommunication between different processes, and not just different classes within one process.

Iterators

The Iterator design pattern is where an iterator is used to traverse a container. In PHP, a class is traversable using the `foreach` construct if it ultimately inherits the Traversable interface. Unfortunately, this is an abstract base interface, you can't implement it alone (unless you're writing in the PHP core itself). Instead, you must instead implement interfaces called `Iterator` or `IteratorAggregate`. By implementing either of these interfaces you make a class iterable and traversable using `foreach`.

`Iterator` and `IteratorAggregate` interfaces are very similar, except the `IteratorAggregate` interface creates an external iterator. `IteratorAggregate` as an interface only requires outlines one method, `getIterator`. This method has to return an instance of the `ArrayIterator` interface.

IteratorAggregate

Let's suppose we want to create an implementation of this interface, which will iterate through various times.

Firstly, let's start off with a basic implementation of the `IternatorAggregate` class to understand how it works:

```php
<?php

class timeIterator implements IteratorAggregate {

  public function getIterator()
  {
    return new ArrayIterator(array(
      'property1' => 1,
      'property2' => 2,
      'property4' => 3
    ));
  }
}
```

We can iterate through this class as follows:

```php
<?php

$time = new timeIterator;

foreach($time as $key => $value) {
  var_dump($key, $value);
  echo "n";
}
```

The output of this is as follows:

I've modified this script so that it takes a `time` value and calculates various values either side and makes them iterable:

```php
<?php

class timeIterator implements IteratorAggregate
{

  public function __construct(int $time)
  {
    $this->weekAgo    = $time - 604800;
    $this->yesterday  = $time - 86400;
    $this->now        = $time;
    $this->tomorrow   = $time + 86400;
    $this->nextWeek   = $time + 604800;
  }

  public function getIterator()
  {
```

```
        return new ArrayIterator($this);
    }
}

$time = new timeIterator(time());

foreach ($time as $key => $value) {
  var_dump($key, $value);
  echo "n";
}
```

The output of this script is as follows:

Iterator

Let's suppose we want to create an implementation of this interface that will iterate through various times.

The many iterators of PHP

Previously, we've explored some functions in the **SPL (Standard PHP Library)**, which is a collection of interfaces and classes that exist to solve common problems. Given this aim, they share a common aim with design patterns, but they both aim to solve these problems in different ways. No external libraries are needed to build this extension and compile in PHP 7; indeed, you can't even disable it.

As part of this library, there are a lot of iterators in the SPL. You can find a list of them in the documentation at `http://php.net/manual/en/spl.iterators.php`.

Here's a list of some of these iterators to give you an idea of what you can utilize them for:

- AppendIterator
- ArrayIterator
- CachingIterator
- CallbackFilterIterator
- DirectoryIterator
- EmptyIterator
- FilesystemIterator
- FilterIterator
- GlobIterator
- InfiniteIterator
- IteratorIterator
- LimitIterator
- MultipleIterator
- NoRewindIterator
- ParentIterator
- RecursiveArrayIterator
- RecursiveCachingIterator
- RecursiveCallbackFilterIterator
- RecursiveDirectoryIterator
- RecursiveFilterIterator
- RecursiveIteratorIterator
- RecursiveRegexIterator
- RecursiveTreeIterator
- RegexIterator

Generators

PHP has a great mechanism to create iterators in a compact fashion. This type of iterator comes with some severe limitations; they are forward only and cannot be rewound. Indeed, even to simply start an iterator from the start, you must rebuild the generator. In essence, this is a forward-only iterator.

A function that uses the `yield` keyword instead of the `return` keyword. This will act in the same way as a `return` statement, but it will not stop the execution of that function. A generator function can `yield` data as many times as you please.

When you populate an array with values, those values must be stored in memory which can cause you to exceed your PHP memory limit or require a significant amount of processing time for the generator. When you put the logic in a generator function, that overhead does not exist. The generator function may merely yield as many results as it needs; there's no need to prepopulate an array first.

Here is a simple generator that will `var_dump` a string stating, the generator has started. The function will then generate the first five square numbers while also outputting their place in the series with `var_dump` . It will then finally indicate the generator has ended:

```php
<?php
function squaredNumbers()
{
  var_dump("Generator starts.");
  for ($i = 0; $i < 5; ++$i) {
    var_dump($i . " in series.");
    yield pow($i, 2);
  }
  var_dump("Generator ends.");
}

foreach (squaredNumbers() as $number) {
  var_dump($number);
}
```

The second part of this script loops through this function and runs a `var_dump` string on each number. The output of this is as follows:

```
1  string(17) "Generator starts."
2  string(12) "0 in series."
3  int(0)
4  string(12) "1 in series."
5  int(1)
6  string(12) "2 in series."
7  int(4)
8  string(12) "3 in series."
9  int(9)
10 string(12) "4 in series."
11 int(16)
12 string(15) "Generator ends."
13
```

Let's amend this function slightly.

It is very important to note that if you add a return type to the variable, you can only declare a return type of `Generator`, `Iterator` or `Traversable`, `integer`.

Here is the code:

```php
<?php
function squaredNumbers(int $start, int $end): Generator
{
  for ($i = $start; $i <= $end; ++$i) {
    yield pow($i, 2);
  }
}

foreach (squaredNumbers(1, 5) as $number) {
  var_dump($number);
}
```

The result of this is as follows:

What if we want to yield a key as well as a value? Well, this is fairly easy.

There's something else to mention about generators to those who used them in PHP 5: in PHP 5, when you want to simultaneously yield a variable while setting it to a variable, you must wrap the yield statement in brackets. This restriction does not exist in PHP 7.

This works in PHP 5 and 7:

```
$data = (yield $value);
```

This only works in PHP 7:

```
$data = yield $value;
```

Let's suppose we want to amend our generator so that it yields a key-value result. Here's what the code looks like:

```php
<?php

function squaredNumbers(int $start, int $end): Generator
{
  for ($i = $start; $i <= $end; ++$i) {
    yield $i => pow($i, 2);
  }
}

foreach (squaredNumbers(1, 5) as $key => $number) {
  var_dump([$key, $number]);
}
```

When we test this, we will `var_dump` a two-dimensional array containing a key-value store of whatever the generator has yielded in a given iteration.

Here is the output:

```
array(2) {
  [0]=>
  int(1)
  [1]=>
  int(1)
}
array(2) {
  [0]=>
  int(2)
  [1]=>
  int(4)
}
array(2) {
  [0]=>
  int(3)
  [1]=>
  int(9)
}
array(2) {
  [0]=>
  int(4)
  [1]=>
  int(16)
}
array(2) {
  [0]=>
  int(5)
  [1]=>
  int(25)
}
```

Just a few other tips, a yield statement with no variable (like the one shown in the succeding command) will simply yield `null`:

```
yield;
```

You may also use `yield from` which will yield the inner values of any given generator.

Let's suppose we have an array of two values:

```
[1, 2]
```

When we use `yield from` to yield an array of two values we get the inner values of the array. Let me demonstrate this:

```php
<?php

function innerGenerator()
{
   yield from [1, 2];
}

foreach (innerGenerator() as $number) {
   var_dump($number);
}
```

This will display the following output:

However, now let's alter this script so that it uses `yield` instead of `yield from`:

```php
<?php

function innerGenerator()
{
   yield [1, 2];
}

foreach (innerGenerator() as $number) {
   var_dump($number);
}
```

We will now see that instead of merely just the inner values of the array, we get the outer container too:

```
1  array(2) {
2    [0]=>
3    int(1)
4    [1]=>
5    int(2)
6  }
7
```

Template Method design pattern

The Template Method design pattern is used to create a group of subclasses that have to execute a similar group of behaviors.

This design pattern consists of a Template Method, which is an abstract class. Concrete subclasses can override the methods within the abstract class. The Template Method consists of a skeleton of an algorithm; the subclasses can use overriding to change the concrete behavior of the algorithm.

As such, this is an incredibly simple design pattern to use; it encourages loose coupling while also controlling at what points subclassing is permitted. Thus, it is more fine-grained than simple polymorphic behavior.

Consider the following abstraction of a `Pasta` class:

```php
<?php

abstract class Pasta
{
  public function __construct(bool $cheese = true)
  {
    $this->cheese = $cheese;
  }
```

```php
  public function cook()
  {

    var_dump('Cooked pasta.');

    $this->boilPasta();
    $this->addSauce();
    $this->addMeat();

    if ($this->cheese) {
      $this->addCheese();
    }
  }

  public function boilPasta(): bool
  {
    return true;
  }


  public abstract function addSauce(): bool;

  public abstract function addMeat(): bool;

  public abstract function addCheese(): bool;

}
```

There is a simple constructor for whether the pasta should contain cheese or not, and a `cook` function that runs the cooking algorithm.

Note that the functions to add various ingredients are abstracted away; in subclasses, we implement these methods with the required behavior.

Suppose we want to make meatball pasta. We can implement this abstract class as follows:

```php
<?php

class MeatballPasta extends Pasta
{

  public function addSauce(): bool
  {
    var_dump("Added tomato sauce");

    return true;
  }
```

```
public function addMeat(): bool
{
  var_dump("Added meatballs.");

  return true;

}

public function addCheese(): bool
{
  var_dump("Added cheese.");

  return true;
}

}
```

We can sample this code using the following script in our index.php file:

```
<?php

require_once('Pasta.php');
require_once('MeatballPasta.php');

var_dump("Meatball pasta");
$dish = new MeatballPasta(true);
$dish->cook();
```

Thanks to all the var_dump variables in the various functions displaying various status messages, we can see an output like this:

Now, suppose we want to make a vegan recipe instead. We can utilize the same abstraction in a different context.

This time when it comes to adding meat or cheese, those functions do nothing; they can return `false` or a `null` value:

```php
<?php

class VeganPasta extends Pasta
{

  public function addSauce(): bool
  {
    var_dump("Added tomato sauce");

    return true;
  }

  public function addMeat(): bool
  {
    return false;
  }

  public function addCheese(): bool
  {
    return false;
  }

}
```

Let's amend our `index.php` file to represent this behavior:

```php
<?php

require_once('Pasta.php');
require_once('MeatballPasta.php');

var_dump("Meatball pasta");
$dish = new MeatballPasta(true);
$dish->cook();

var_dump("");
var_dump("Vegan pasta");
require_once('VeganPasta.php');

$dish = new VeganPasta(true);
$dish->cook();
```

The output is as follows:

```
 1   string(14)  "Meatball pasta"
 2   string(13)  "Cooked pasta."
 3   string(18)  "Added tomato sauce"
 4   string(16)  "Added meatballs."
 5   string(13)  "Added cheese."
 6   string(0)   ""
 7   string(11)  "Vegan pasta"
 8   string(13)  "Cooked pasta."
 9   string(18)  "Added tomato sauce"
10
```

This design pattern is simple and easy to work with, but it fundamentally allows you to abstract your algorithm design and delegate that responsibility to subclasses where you want to.

Chain of Responsibility

Suppose we have a group of objects that together are meant to solve a problem. When one object can't solve a problem, we want the object to send the task to a different object in a given chain. This is what the Chain of Responsibility design pattern is used for.

In order to get this to work, we need a handler, which will be our `Chain` interface. The various objects in the chain will all implement this `Chain` interface.

Let's start with a simple example; an associate can purchase an asset for less than $100, a manager can purchase something for less than $500.

Our abstraction for the `Purchaser` interface looks like this:

```php
<?php

interface Purchaser
{
  public function setNextPurchaser(Purchaser $nextPurchaser): bool;

  public function buy($price): bool;
}
```

Our first implementation is the `Associate` class. Quite simply, we implement the `setNextPurchaser` function so that it will set the `nextPurchaser` class property to the next object in the chain.

When we call the `buy` function, if the price is within range, the associate will purchase it. If not, the next purchaser in the chain will purchase it:

```php
<?php

class AssociatePurchaser implements Purchaser
{
  public function setNextPurchaser(Purchaser $nextPurchaser): bool
  {
    $this->nextPurchaser = $nextPurchaser;
    return true;
  }

  public function buy($price): bool
  {
    if ($price < 100) {
      var_dump("Associate purchased");
      return true;
    } else {
      if (isset($this->nextPurchaser)) {
        reurn $this->nextPurchaser->buy($price);
      } else {
        var_dump("Could not buy");
        return false;
      }
    }
  }
}
```

Our `Manager` class is exactly the same; we just allow the manager to purchase assets which are under $500. In reality, when you apply this pattern you wouldn't just duplicate a class as your class would have different logic; this example is just an incredibly simple implementation.

Here's the code:

```php
<?php

class ManagerPurchaser implements Purchaser
{
  public function setNextPurchaser(Purchaser $nextPurchaser): bool
  {
    $this->nextPurchaser = $nextPurchaser;
    return true;
  }

  public function buy($price): bool
  {
    if ($price < 500) {
      var_dump("Associate purchased");
      return true;
    } else {
      if (isset($this->nextPurchaser)) {
        return $this->nextPurchaser->buy($price);
      } else {
        var_dump("Could not buy");
        return false;
      }
    }
  }
}
```

Let's run a basic purchase from an associate in our `index.php` file.

Firstly, here's the code we put in our `index.php` file:

```php
<?php

require_once('Purchaser.php');
require_once('AssociatePurchaser.php');

$associate = new AssociatePurchaser();

$associate->buy(50);
```

The output of all of this is as follows:

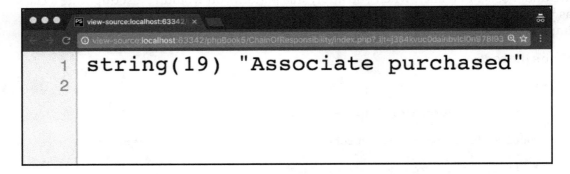

Next, let's test our `Manager` class. We'll amend our purchase price in our `index.php` file and also add our `Manager` class to the chain.

Here's our amended `index.php`:

```php
<?php

require_once('Purchaser.php');
require_once('AssociatePurchaser.php');
require_once('ManagerPurchaser.php');

$associate = new AssociatePurchaser();
$manager = new ManagerPurchaser();

$associate->setNextPurchaser($manager);

$associate->buy(400);
```

This has the following output:

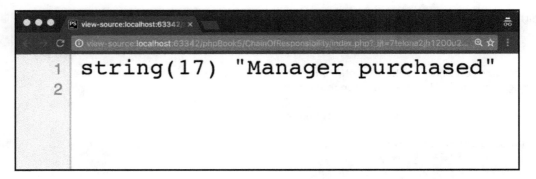

Let's see what happens if we alter the price such that the purchase will fail.

We change the final line on our `index.php` file so the purchase price is now $600:

```php
<?php

require_once('Purchaser.php');
require_once('AssociatePurchaser.php');
require_once('ManagerPurchaser.php');

$associate = new AssociatePurchaser();
$manager = new ManagerPurchaser();

$associate->setNextPurchaser($manager);

$associate->buy(600);
```

This has the following output:

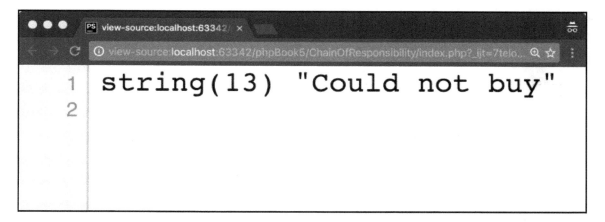

We can now extend this script. Let's add `DirectorPurchaser` and `BoardPurchaser` so we can make purchases at a higher cost.

We'll create a `DirectorPurchaser` who can buy under $10,000.

This class is as follows:

```php
<?php

class DirectorPurchaser implements Purchaser
{
    public function setNextPurchaser(Purchaser $nextPurchaser): bool
    {
```

```php
      $this->nextPurchaser = $nextPurchaser;
      return true;
  }

  public function buy($price): bool
  {
    if ($price < 10000) {
      var_dump("Director purchased");
      return true;
    } else {
      if (isset($this->nextPurchaser)) {
        return $this->nextPurchaser->buy($price);
      } else {
        var_dump("Could not buy");
        return false;
      }
    }
  }
}
```

Let's do the same for a `BoardPurchaser` class who can purchase below $100,000:

```php
<?php

class BoardPurchaser implements Purchaser
{
  public function setNextPurchaser(Purchaser $nextPurchaser): bool
  {
    $this->nextPurchaser = $nextPurchaser;
    return true;
  }

  public function buy($price): bool
  {
    if ($price < 100000) {
      var_dump("Board purchased");
      return true;
    } else {
      if (isset($this->nextPurchaser)) {
        return $this->nextPurchaser->buy($price);
      } else {
        var_dump("Could not buy");
        return false;
      }
    }
  }
}
```

Now we can update our `index.php` script to require the new classes, instantiate them, and then bind everything together in a chain. Finally, we'll attempt to run a purchase by calling the first in the chain.

Here's the script:

```php
<?php

require_once('Purchaser.php');
require_once('AssociatePurchaser.php');
require_once('ManagerPurchaser.php');
require_once('DirectorPurchaser.php');
require_once('BoardPurchaser.php');

$associate = new AssociatePurchaser();
$manager = new ManagerPurchaser();
$director = new DirectorPurchaser();
$board = new BoardPurchaser();

$associate->setNextPurchaser($manager);
$manager->setNextPurchaser($director);
$director->setNextPurchaser($board);

$associate->buy(11000);
```

Here's the output of this script:

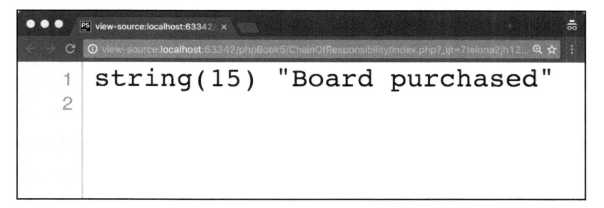

This allows us to traverse a chain of objects to process data. This is particularly useful when dealing with tree data structures (for example, an XML tree). This can act in a launch-and-leave manner where we can lower the overhead of handling iterating through the chain.

Moreover, the chain is loosely coupled, data is passed through a chain until it is processed. Any object can be chained to any other object in any order.

Strategy design pattern

The Strategy design pattern exists to allow us to alter the behavior of an object at runtime.

Let's suppose we have a class that will raise a number to a power, but at runtime we want to alter whether we square or cube a number.

Let's start off by defining an interface a function that will raise a number to a given power:

```php
<?php

interface Power
{
    public function raise(int $number): int;
}
```

We can accordingly define classes to `Square` and also `Cube` a given number by implementing the interface.

Here's our `Square` class:

```php
<?php

class Square implements Power
{
    public function raise(int $number): int
    {
        return pow($number, 2);
    }
}
```

And let's define our `Cube` class:

```php
<?php

class Cube implements Power
{
    public function raise(int $number): int
```

```
    {
        return pow($number, 3);
    }
}
```

We can now build a class that will essentially use one of these classes to process a number.

Here's the class:

```php
<?php

class RaiseNumber
{
    public function __construct(Power $strategy)
    {
        $this->strategy = $strategy;
    }

    public function raise(int $number)
    {
        return $this->strategy->raise($number);
    }
}
```

Now we can demonstrate this whole setup using an index.php file:

```php
<?php

require_once('Power.php');
require_once('Square.php');
require_once('Cube.php');
require_once('RaiseNumber.php');


$processor = new RaiseNumber(new Square());

var_dump($processor->raise(5));
```

The output is as expected, 5^2 is 25.

Here's the output:

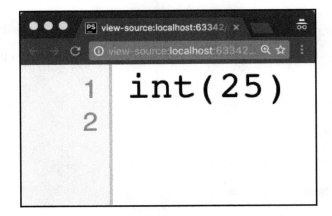

We can swap the `Square` object with the `Cube` object in our `index.php` file:

```php
<?php

require_once('Power.php');
require_once('Square.php');
require_once('Cube.php');
require_once('RaiseNumber.php');


$processor = new RaiseNumber(new Cube());

var_dump($processor->raise(5));
```

Here's the output of the updated script:

So far so good; but the reason that this is great is the fact that we can dynamically add logic that actually changes the operation of the class.

Here's a rather crude demonstration of all this:

```php
<?php

require_once('Power.php');
require_once('Square.php');
require_once('Cube.php');
require_once('RaiseNumber.php');

if (isset($_GET['n'])) {
  $number = $_GET['n'];
} else {
  $number = 0;
}

if ($number < 5) {
  $power = new Cube();
} else {
  $power = new Square();
}

$processor = new RaiseNumber($power);

var_dump($processor->raise($number));
```

So just to demonstrate this, let's run the script with the *n*GET variable set to 4, which should cube the number 4, giving an output of 64:

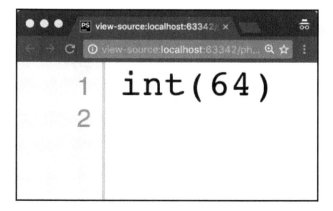

Now if we pass through the number 6, we expect the script to square the number 6, giving an output of 36:

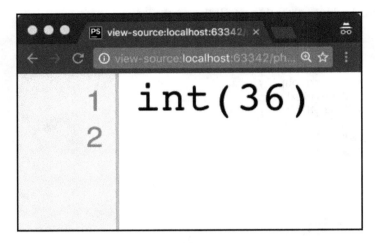

In this design pattern, we have done a lot:

- We defined a family of algorithms, bound by one common interface
- These algorithms are interchangeable; they can be swapped in and out without affecting the client implementation
- We encapsulated each algorithm within a class

Now we can vary the algorithm independently from the clients that use it.

Specification design pattern

The Specification design pattern is incredibly powerful. Here, I will attempt to provide a high-level overview of it, but there is plenty to explore; I highly recommend the paper *Specifications* by *Eric Evans* and *Martin Fowler* if you are interested in learning more.

This design pattern is used to codify business rules that state something about an object. They tell us whether an object satisfies some business criteria or not.

We can use them in the following ways:

- To make assertions about an object, for *validation*
- To fetch a *selection* of objects from a given collection
- To specify how an object can be created by *building to order*

In this example, we're going to build Specification to query

Let's take the following objects:

```php
<?php

$workers = array();

$workers['A'] = new StdClass();
$workers['A']->title = "Developer";
$workers['A']->department = "Engineering";
$workers['A']->salary = 50000;

$workers['B'] = new StdClass();
$workers['B']->title = "Data Analyst";
$workers['B']->department = "Engineering";
$workers['B']->salary = 30000;

$workers['C'] = new StdClass();
$workers['C']->title = "Personal Assistant";
$workers['C']->department = "CEO";
$workers['C']->salary = 25000;

The workers array will look like this if we var_dump it:
array(3) {
  ["A"]=>
  object(stdClass)#1 (3) {
    ["title"]=>
    string(9) "Developer"
    ["department"]=>
    string(11) "Engineering"
    ["salary"]=>
    int(50000)
  }
  ["B"]=>
  object(stdClass)#2 (3) {
    ["title"]=>
    string(12) "Data Analyst"
    ["department"]=>
    string(11) "Engineering"
    ["salary"]=>
    int(30000)
  }
  ["C"]=>
  object(stdClass)#3 (3) {
    ["title"]=>
    string(18) "Personal Assistant"
    ["department"]=>
```

```
      string(3) "CEO"
      ["salary"]=>
      int(25000)
   }
}
```

Let's kick things off with an `EmployeeSpecification` interface; this is the interface that all our specifications will need to implement. Be sure to replace `StdClass` with the type of object you're dealing with (for example, employee, or the name of the class you instantiated the object from).

Here's the code:

```php
<?php

interface EmployeeSpecification
{
  public function isSatisfiedBy(StdClass $customer): bool;
}
```

It's time to write an implementation called `EmployeeIsEngineer`:

```php
<?php

class EmployeeIsEngineer implements EmployeeSpecification
{
  public function isSatisfiedBy(StdClass $customer): bool
  {
    if ($customer->department === "Engineering") {
      return true;
    }
    return false;
  }
}
```

We can then iterate through our workers to check which ones meet the criteria we outlined:

```php
$isEngineer = new EmployeeIsEngineer();

foreach ($workers as $id => $worker) {
  if ($isEngineer->isSatisfiedBy($worker)) {
    var_dump($id);
  }
}
```

Let's put this all together in our `index.php` file:

```php
<?php

require_once('EmployeeSpecification.php');
require_once('EmployeeIsEngineer.php');

$workers = array();

$workers['A'] = new StdClass();
$workers['A']->title = "Developer";
$workers['A']->department = "Engineering";
$workers['A']->salary = 50000;

$workers['B'] = new StdClass();
$workers['B']->title = "Data Analyst";
$workers['B']->department = "Engineering";
$workers['B']->salary = 30000;

$workers['C'] = new StdClass();
$workers['C']->title = "Personal Assistant";
$workers['C']->department = "CEO";
$workers['C']->salary = 25000;

$isEngineer = new EmployeeIsEngineer();

foreach ($workers as $id => $worker) {
  if ($isEngineer->isSatisfiedBy($worker)) {
    var_dump($id);
  }
}
```

Here's the output of this script:

Composite Specifications allow you to combine specifications. By using the AND, NOT, OR and NOR operators you are able to build their respective functions into different specification classes.

Similarly, you can also fetch objects using a specification.

This code gets more complicated as you go further, but you understand the gist. Indeed, the paper by Eric Evans and Martin Fowler I mentioned at the start of the section goes into some far more complicated arrangements.

Either way, this design pattern fundamentally allows us to encapsulate business logic to state something about an object. It is an incredibly powerful design pattern and I would highly encourage studying it more deeply.

Scheduled Task pattern

A scheduled task fundamentally consists of three things: the task itself, the jobs that do the scheduling by defining when the task that is being run and when it is permitted to run, and finally, the job registry that executes this job.

Commonly, these are implemented by using cron on Linux servers. You add a line to the `configuration` file using the following configuration syntax:

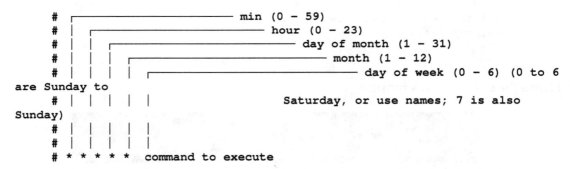

```
# ┌─────────────────────── min (0 - 59)
# │ ┌───────────────────── hour (0 - 23)
# │ │ ┌─────────────────── day of month (1 - 31)
# │ │ │ ┌───────────────── month (1 - 12)
# │ │ │ │ ┌─────────────── day of week (0 - 6) (0 to 6
  are Sunday to
# │ │ │ │ │               Saturday, or use names; 7 is also
  Sunday)
# │ │ │ │ │
# │ │ │ │ │
# * * * * *  command to execute
```

You can ordinarily edit the `cron` file by running `crontab -e` in the command line. You can schedule any Linux command using this pattern. Here's a cronjob that will run a PHP script at 20:00 (8 PM) every day:

```
0 20 * * * /usr/bin/php /opt/test.php
```

These are very simple to run to implement, but here are some guidelines to help guide you when you create them:

- Don't expose your cronjobs to the Internet.
- When you run the task, the task shouldn't check the criteria as to whether it needs to run or not. This test should be outside the task.
- The task should only do the scheduled activity it's intended to do and not perform any other purpose.
- Beware of the Database-as-IPC pattern we discussed in `Chapter 7`, Refactoring.

You can put whatever you want in the task (within reason). You may find an asynchronous execution the best route. Icicle is a great PHP library for performing async behavior. You can find the documentation online at `https://icicle.io/`.

Where our task needs several tasks to be done in a specific order, you may benefit from using the Composite design pattern we discussed in the Structural design patterns section and calling a single task that uses this pattern to call other tasks using this pattern.

Summary

In this chapter, we've covered some patterns that identify common communication patterns between objects.

We covered how the Observer pattern can be used to update observers on the status of a given subject. Additionally, we learned how the standard PHP library contains functionality that can help us with this.

We then went on to cover how we can implement iterators in many different ways in PHP, using various interfaces in the PHP core alongside utilizing the generator function.

We went on to discuss how the Template pattern can define an algorithm skeleton that we can dynamically adapt in a more stringent way than standard polymorphism. We covered the Chain of Responsibility pattern, which allows us link together objects in a chain to execute various functionality. The Strategy pattern taught us how we can alter behavior of code at runtime. I then introduced the basics of the Specification pattern and how advanced the functionality in it is. Finally, we revised the Scheduled Task pattern and how it can be implemented using cron on Linux.

These design patterns are some of the most critical ones for developers. Communication between objects is vital in many projects and these patterns can really aid us in this communication.

In the next chapter, we'll look at Architectural patterns and how these can help you with the software architecture tasks that arise and how these can help you address the broader software engineering challenges you may face (though they may not be technically considered design patterns themselves).

6
Architectural Patterns

Architectural patterns, sometimes referred to as an architectural style, provide solutions to recurring problems in software architecture.

Though similar to software design patterns, they have a broader scope, addressing various issues in software engineering as opposed to simply the development of software itself.

In this chapter we will cover the following topics:

- Model-View-Controller (MVC)
- Service-oriented architecture
- Microservices
- Asynchronous queuing
- Message Queue pattern

Model-View-Controller (MVC)

MVC is the most common type of Architectural pattern that PHP developers encounter. Fundamentally, MVC is an Architectural pattern for implementing user interfaces.

It largely works around the following methodology:

- **Model**: This supplies the data to the application, whether it's from a MySQL database or any other data store.
- **Controller**: A Controller is essentially where the business logic is. The Controller handles whatever queries the View provides, using the Model to assist it in this behavior.
- **View**: The actual content that is supplied to the end-user. This commonly is an HTML template.

Business logic for one interaction isn't strictly separated from another interaction. There is no formal separation between the different classes of an application.

It is critical to consider that the MVC pattern is principally a UI pattern, so it doesn't scale well throughout an application. That said, the rendering of UIs is increasingly being done via JavaScript applications, a single page JavaScript HTML app that simply consumes a RESTful APIs.

If you're using JavaScript, you may use a framework such as Backbone.js (Model-View-Presenter), React.js, or Angular to communicate with your backend APIs, though this will of course, require a JavaScript enabled web browser, which some of us can take for granted from our users.

In the event you exist in an environment where you cannot use a JavaScript app and must instead serve rendered HTML, it often is a good idea for your MVC app to simply consume a REST API. The REST API performs all the business logic, but the rendering of markup is done in the MVC app. Although this increases complexity, it offers a greater separation of responsibilities and as a result, you don't have HTML being merged with core business logic. That said, even within this REST API you need some form of separation of concerns, you need to be able to separate, the rendering of the markup from the actual business logic.

A key element to choosing an Architectural pattern suitable for an app is whether the complexity is appropriate for the size of the app. Thus, choosing an MVC framework should also be based on the complexity of the app itself and its intended complexity later on.

Given the growth of infrastructure as code, it is possible to deploy the infrastructure of multiple web services in an entirely orchestrated fashion. Indeed, using containerization technology such as Docker, it is possible to deploy multiple architectures (such as an MVC application with a separate API service) with little overhead (no need to spin up a new server for each service).

Separation of concerns is a vital trait when developing great architectures, which includes separating UI from business logic.

When thinking in terms of an MVC pattern, it is important to remember the interactions as follows:

- The Model stores data, which is retrieved according to the query put by the Model and displayed by the View
- The View generates outputs based on changes to the Model
- The Controller sends the command to update the Model's state; it can also update the View associated to it to alter how a given Model is presented

Or, it is commonly expressed using the following diagram:

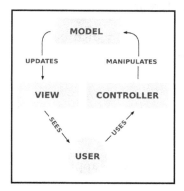

Don't use an MVC framework for the sake of using one, understand why they exist and where they can fit well into a use case. Remember that when you take on a bloated framework with lots of functionality, you are taking responsibility for maintaining the whole thing going forward.

Pulling in the components as you need them (that is, through Composer) is a far more practical approach to developing software with considerable business logic.

Service-oriented architecture

Service-oriented architectures largely consist of business logic in services that communicate with data repositories.

These services can be derived in different forms to build applications. These applications adopt these services in different formats to build various applications. Consider the services as Lego blocks that can be put together to build an application in a given format.

This description is rather crude; let me clarify further:

- Boundaries for services are explicit (they may separate web services on different domains, and so on.)
- Services can inter-communicate using a common communication protocol (for example all use RESTful APIs)
- Services are autonomous (they are decoupled and not related to another service in any way)
- The message processing mechanism and the schema are understandable by every other microservice (and therefore are often the same), but the programming environment can be different

Service-oriented architectures are inherently distributed, thus they can have higher up-front complexity than other architectures.

Microservices

A microservices architecture can be considered a subset of service-oriented architectures.

Fundamentally, microservices form complex applications by composing them of small independent process which intercommunicate over a language-agnostic API that makes each services accessible to each other. Microservices can be individually deployed as services.

In microservices, the business logic is separated into self-contained loosely-coupled services. A key tenet of microservices is that each database should have their own database, which is vital to ensure that the microservices do not become tightly coupled to each other.

By reducing the complexity of a single service, we can aim to reduce the amount of points at which this service will fail. In theory, by having a single service comply with the Single Responsibility Principle, it is easier to debug and reduce chances of failure in our application as a whole.

In computer science, the CAP theorem dictates that it is impossible to guarantee consistency, availability, and partition tolerance concurrently in a given distributed computer system.

Imagine two distributed databases both containing the e-mail address of a user. If we want to update this e-mail address, there is no way we can do so in a way that is instantaneously available across both databases with the e-mail consistently updated at the same time while not bringing the two datasets back together. In a distributed system we would have to either delay the access to the data to validate the data is consistent or present a non-updated copy of the data.

This makes traditional database transaction difficult. Thus, the best way to address data handling in a microservices architecture is to use an eventually consistent, event-driven architecture.

Each service publishes an event whenever there is a change, and other services may subscribe to this. When an event is received, the data is accordingly updated. Thus, the application is able to maintain data consistency across multiple services without needing to use distributed transactions.

In order to see how such an architecture for inter-process communication can be implemented for communication between microservices, please see the *Message Queue pattern (Getting started with RabbitMQ)* section in this chapter.

In this situation, one simple way to mitigate against this restriction is simply by using a time verification system in order to verify the data is consistent. Thus, we surrender availability for consistency and partition tolerance.

If you can foresee this as a problem in a given microservices architecture, it is often best to group the services that need to satisfy the CAP theorem together into a single service.

Let's consider a pizza delivery web application that consists of the following microservices:

- User
- Deals
- Recipe
- Cart
- Billing
- Payments
- Restaurant
- Delivery
- Pizza
- Reviews
- Frontend microservice

In this example, we could have the following user journey:

1. The user is authenticated using the User microservice.
2. The user can select offers using the Deals microservice.
3. The user selects the pizza they want to order using the Recipe microservice.
4. Selected pizza(s) are added to the cart using the Cart microservice.
5. Billing credentials optimated through the Billing microservice.
6. The user pays using the Payments microservice.
7. The order is sent to the restaurant using the Restaurant microservice.
8. When the Restaurant has cooked the food, the Delivery microservice sends a driver to collect the food and deliver it.
9. Once the Delivery microservice indicates the food has been delivered, the user is invited to complete a review using the Review microservice (which notifies the user using the User microservice).
10. The web front of this is wrapped together using the Frontend microservice.

The Frontend microservice can simply be a microservice that consumes the other microservices and presents the content to the web frontend. This frontend may communicate with the other microservices over REST, perhaps implemented in a JavaScript client in the browser, or a PHP app that merely acts as a consumer of other microservice APIs.

Either way, it is often a good idea to place a gateway between the frontend consumer of your API and the backend. This allows us to put some middleware before communication to microservices is ascertained; for example, we can use the gateway to query the User microservice to check that a user is authorized before allowing access to the Cart microservice.

If you're using JavaScript to communicate directly with the microservices, you may find cross-origin issues when your web frontend tries to communicate with microservices on different hostnames/ports; a microservice gateway can help prevent this by putting the gateway on the same origin as the web frontend itself.

In exchange for this convenience of a gateway, you'll likely feel the drawbacks in terms of the fact that you will have another system to worry about and additional response time (though you can add caching at the gateway level should you want to improve performance there).

Given the addition of a gateway, our architecture could now look something like this:

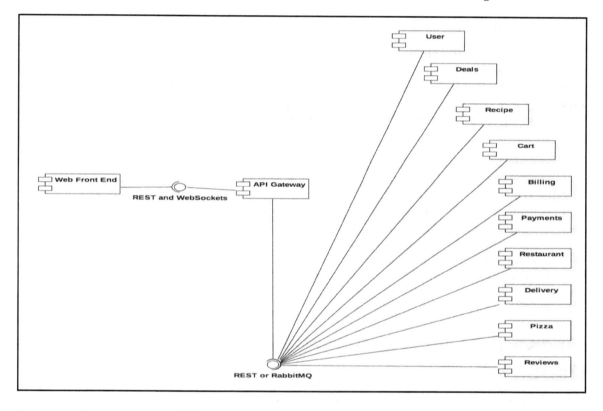

Increasingly emerging in PHP are micro-frameworks such as Lumen, Silex, and Slim; these are API-oriented frameworks that make it easy to build microservices to support our applications. That said, you may often be better to adopt an even more lightweight approach and merely pull in the components you require through Composer as and when you need them.

Remember that adding another technology or framework adds additional complexity to your overall situation. Think not only of the technical reasons of implementing a new solution but also how this will benefit the customer and the architecture. Microservices aren't an excuse to add unnecessary complexity: *Keep It Simple, Stupid.*

Asynchronous queueing

Message queues provide an asynchronous communication protocol. In an asynchronous communication protocol, the sender and the receiver need not interact with the message queue simultaneously.

Typical HTTP, on the other hand, is a synchronous communication protocol, meaning that the client is blocked until the operation is completed.

Consider this; you call someone on the phone, then you wait for the phone to ring and the person you talk to listens to whatever you have to say then and there. At the end of the communication you say *goodbye* and that is acknowledged by someone on the other end saying *goodbye* back. This can be considered synchronous as you don't do anything until you get a response from the person you're communicating with to end the communication.

However, if you were to send a text message to someone instead, after you send that message you can go off and do whatever behavior you please; you can receive a message in return to the one you sent when they want to communicate back to you. While someone is drafting the response to send back, you can go off and do whatever you want. While you don't communicate directly with the sender, you do still maintain synchronous communication with your phone, which notifies you when you get a new message (or simply check your phone every few minutes); but the communication with the other party itself is asynchronous. Neither party needs to know anything about the other party, they just merely are looking out for their own text messages in order to communicate with each other.

Message Queue pattern (Getting started with RabbitMQ)

RabbitMQ is a message broker; it accepts and forwards messages. Here, let's configure it so that we can send messages from one PHP script to another.

Imagine we are giving a package to a courier in order for them to give to the client; RabbitMQ is the courier, while the scripts are the individuals receiving and sending the packages respectively.

As the first step, let's install RabbitMQ; I'm going to demonstrate this on an Ubuntu 14.04 system.

To start with, we need to add the RabbitMQ APT repository to our
/etc/apt/sources.list.d folder. This can fortunately be actioned with a command, like
this:

```
echo 'deb http://www.rabbitmq.com/debian/ testing main' | sudo tee
/etc/apt/sources.list.d/rabbitmq.list
```

Note that the repository may be liable to change; if it does, you can find the latest details at
https://www.rabbitmq.com/install-debian.html.

We can optionally also add the RabbitMQ public key to the trusted key list to avoid any
warnings indicating packages are unsigned when we install or upgrade the packages
through the apt command:

```
wget -O- https://www.rabbitmq.com/rabbitmq-release-signing-key.asc | sudo
apt-key add -
```

So far, so good:

```
junade — root@junade-test: ~ — ssh root@178.62.40.19 — 80×19
[root@junade-test:~# echo 'deb http://www.rabbitmq.com/debian/ testing main' | su
do tee /etc/apt/sources.list.d/rabbitmq.list
deb http://www.rabbitmq.com/debian/ testing main
root@junade-test:~# wget -O- https://www.rabbitmq.com/rabbitmq-release-signing-k
ey.asc | sudo apt-key add -
--2016-07-01 19:28:56--  https://www.rabbitmq.com/rabbitmq-release-signing-key.a
sc
Resolving www.rabbitmq.com (www.rabbitmq.com)... 192.240.153.117
Connecting to www.rabbitmq.com (www.rabbitmq.com)|192.240.153.117|:443... connec
ted.
HTTP request sent, awaiting response... 200 OK
Length: 3187 (3.1K) [text/plain]
Saving to: 'STDOUT'

100%[====================================>] 3,187       --.-K/s    in 0s

2016-07-01 19:28:56 (154 MB/s) - written to stdout [3187/3187]

OK
```

Next, let's just run an apt-get update command to fetch the packages from the new
repository we've included. After this is done we can get around to installing the package we
need using the apt-get install rabbitmq-server command:

```
                  junade — root@junade-test: ~ — ssh root@178.62.40.19 — 80×19
Hit http://mirrors.digitalocean.com trusty/main amd64 Packages
Hit http://mirrors.digitalocean.com trusty/restricted amd64 Packages
Hit http://mirrors.digitalocean.com trusty/universe amd64 Packages
Hit http://mirrors.digitalocean.com trusty/multiverse amd64 Packages
Hit http://mirrors.digitalocean.com trusty/main i386 Packages
Hit http://mirrors.digitalocean.com trusty/restricted i386 Packages
Hit http://mirrors.digitalocean.com trusty/universe i386 Packages
Hit http://mirrors.digitalocean.com trusty/multiverse i386 Packages
Hit http://mirrors.digitalocean.com trusty/main Translation-en
Hit http://mirrors.digitalocean.com trusty/multiverse Translation-en
Hit http://mirrors.digitalocean.com trusty/restricted Translation-en
Hit http://mirrors.digitalocean.com trusty/universe Translation-en
Ign http://mirrors.digitalocean.com trusty/main Translation-en_US
Ign http://mirrors.digitalocean.com trusty/multiverse Translation-en_US
Ign http://mirrors.digitalocean.com trusty/restricted Translation-en_US
Ign http://mirrors.digitalocean.com trusty/universe Translation-en_US
Fetched 1,469 kB in 11s (124 kB/s)
Reading package lists... Done
root@junade-test:~# sudo apt-get install rabbitmq-server
```

Be sure to accept the various prompts when asked:

```
                  junade — root@junade-test: ~ — ssh root@178.62.40.19 — 80×19
  erlang-inets erlang-mnesia erlang-nox erlang-odbc erlang-os-mon
  erlang-parsetools erlang-percept erlang-public-key erlang-runtime-tools
  erlang-snmp erlang-ssl erlang-ssl erlang-syntax-tools erlang-tools
  erlang-webtool erlang-xmerl libltdl7 libodbc1 libsctp1 lksctp-tools socat
Suggested packages:
  erlang erlang-manpages erlang-doc xsltproc fop erlang-ic-java
  erlang-observer libmyodbc odbc-postgresql tdsodbc unixodbc-bin
The following NEW packages will be installed:
  erlang-asn1 erlang-base erlang-corba erlang-crypto erlang-diameter
  erlang-edoc erlang-eldap erlang-erl-docgen erlang-eunit erlang-ic
  erlang-inets erlang-mnesia erlang-nox erlang-odbc erlang-os-mon
  erlang-parsetools erlang-percept erlang-public-key erlang-runtime-tools
  erlang-snmp erlang-ssl erlang-ssl erlang-syntax-tools erlang-tools
  erlang-webtool erlang-xmerl libltdl7 libodbc1 libsctp1 lksctp-tools
  rabbitmq-server socat
0 upgraded, 32 newly installed, 0 to remove and 0 not upgraded.
Need to get 24.2 MB of archives.
After this operation, 42.5 MB of additional disk space will be used.
Do you want to continue? [Y/n] Y
```

After installation, you may run `rabbitmqctl status` to check the status of the application to check it's running OK:

```
[root@junade-test:~# rabbitmqctl status
Status of node 'rabbit@junade-test' ...
[{pid,2879},
 {running_applications,[{rabbit,"RabbitMQ","3.6.2"},
                        {mnesia,"MNESIA  CXC 138 12","4.11"},
                        {os_mon,"CPO  CXC 138 46","2.2.14"},
                        {rabbit_common,[],"3.6.2"},
                        {ranch,"Socket acceptor pool for TCP protocols.",
                               "1.2.1"},
                        {xmerl,"XML parser","1.3.5"},
                        {sasl,"SASL  CXC 138 11","2.3.4"},
                        {stdlib,"ERTS  CXC 138 10","1.19.4"},
                        {kernel,"ERTS  CXC 138 10","2.16.4"}]},
 {os,{unix,linux}},
 {erlang_version,"Erlang R16B03 (erts-5.10.4) [source] [64-bit] [async-threads:6
4] [kernel-poll:true]\n"},
 {memory,[{total,43420872},
          {connection_readers,0},
          {connection_writers,0},
```

Let's make our lives easier for a second. We can use a web GUI to manage RabbitMQ; simply run the following command:

```
rabbitmq-plugins enable rabbitmq_management
```

```
[root@junade-test:~/rabbitmq# rabbitmq-plugins enable rabbitmq_management
The following plugins have been enabled:
  mochiweb
  webmachine
  rabbitmq_web_dispatch
  amqp_client
  rabbitmq_management_agent
  rabbitmq_management

Applying plugin configuration to rabbit@junade-test... started 6 plugins.
root@junade-test:~/rabbitmq#
```

We can now see an admin interface at `<your server IP here>:15672`:

But before we can log in, we're going to have to create some login credentials. In order to do this we're going to have to head back to the command line.

Firstly, we'll need to set a new account with a username of `junade` and a password of `insecurepassword`:

```
rabbitmqctl add_user junade insecurepassword
```

Then we can add some admin privileges:

```
rabbitmqctl set_user_tags junade administrator
rabbitmqctl set_permissions -p / junade ".*" ".*" ".*"
```

Returning to the login page, we can now see our cool admin interface after we enter in these credentials:

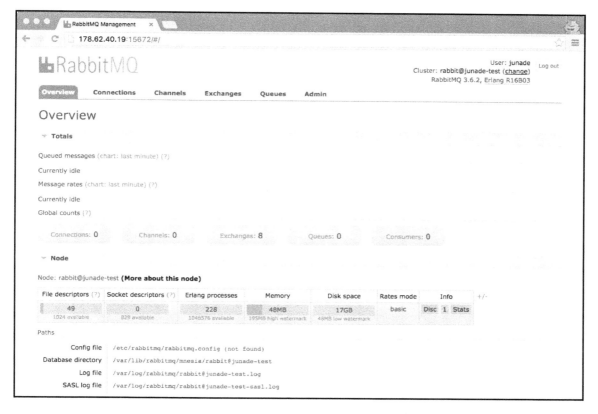

This is the web interface for the RabbitMQ service, accessible through our web browser

Now we can test what we've installed. Let's start off by writing a `composer.json` file for this new project:

```
{
  "require": {
    "php-amqplib/php-amqplib": "2.5.*"
  }
}
```

RabbitMQ uses the **advanced message queuing protocol** (**AMQP**), which is why we're installing a PHP library that will essentially help us communicate with it over this protocol.

Next up, we can write some code to send a message using the RabbitMQ message broker we just installed:

This assumes the port is `5672` and the install is on `localhost`, which may change depending on your circumstances.

Let's write a little PHP script to utilize this:

```php
<?php

require_once(__DIR__ . '/vendor/autoload.php');
use PhpAmqpLib\Connection\AMQPStreamConnection;
use PhpAmqpLib\Message\AMQPMessage;

$connection = new AMQPStreamConnection('localhost', 5672, 'junade',
'insecurepassword');
$channel    = $connection->channel();

$channel->queue_declare(
    'sayHello',      // queue name
    false,           // passive
    true,            // durable
    false,           // exclusive
    false            // autodelete
);

$msg = new AMQPMessage("Hello world!");

$channel->basic_publish(
    $msg,            // message
    '',              // exchange
    'sayHello'       // routing key
);

$channel->close();
$connection->close();

echo "Sent hello world message." . PHP_EOL;
```

So let's break this down a little bit. In the first few lines, we just include the library from the Composer `autoload` and `state` which namespaces we're going to use. When we instantiate the `AMQPStreamConnection` object we actually connect to the message broker; we can then create a new channel object that we then use to declare a new queue on. We declare a queue by calling the `queue_declare` message. The durable option allows messages to survive reboots in RabbitMQ. Finally, we just go ahead and send out our message.

Let's now run this script:

php send.php

The output of this looks like this:

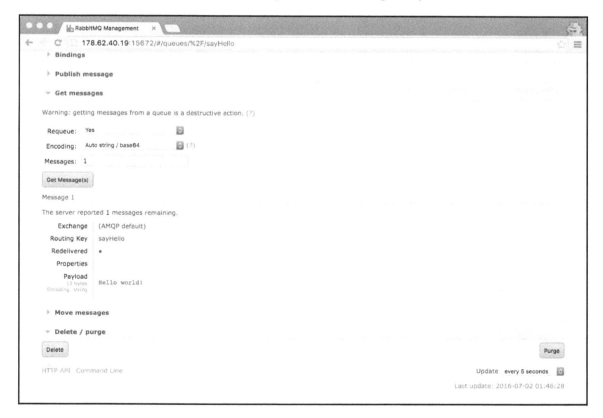

If you now go to the web interface for RabbitMQ, click the queues tab and toggle the **Get Message(s)** dialog; you should be able to pull in the message we just sent to the broker:

Using this web page in the interface, we can extract messages from the queue so we can look at their contents

Of course, this is just half the story. We now need to actually retrieve this message using another app.

Let's write a `receive.php` script:

```php
<?php

require_once(__DIR__ . '/vendor/autoload.php');
use PhpAmqpLib\Connection\AMQPStreamConnection;
use PhpAmqpLib\Message\AMQPMessage;

$connection = new AMQPStreamConnection('localhost', 5672, 'junade',
'insecurepassword');
$channel    = $connection->channel();

$channel->queue_declare(
    'sayHello',      // queue name
    false,           // passive
    false,           // durable
    false,           // exclusive
    false            // autodelete
);

$callback = function ($msg) {
    echo "Received: " . $msg->body . PHP_EOL;
};

$channel->basic_consume(
    'sayHello',                      // queue
    '',                              // consumer tag
    false,                           // no local
    true,                            // no ack
    false,                           // exclusive
    false,                           // no wait
    $callback                        // callback
);

while (count($channel->callbacks)) {
    $channel->wait();
}
```

Note that the first few lines are identical to our sending script; we even re-declare the queue in case this receive script is run before the `send.php` script is run.

Let's run our `receive.php` script:

```
root@junade-test: ~/rabbitmq — ssh root@178.62.40.19      root@junade-test: ~/rabbitmq — ssh root@178.62.40.19

root@junade-test:~/rabbitmq# php recieve.php
```

In another bash Terminal, let's run the `send.php` script a few times:

```
root@junade-test: ~/rabbitmq — ssh root@178.62.40.19   ...   root@junade-test: ~/rabbitmq — ssh root@178.62.40.19

root@junade-test:~/rabbitmq# php send.php
Sent hello world message.
root@junade-test:~/rabbitmq# php send.php
Sent hello world message.
root@junade-test:~/rabbitmq# php send.php
Sent hello world message.
root@junade-test:~/rabbitmq#
```

Accordingly, in the `receive.php` Terminal tab, we can now see we've received the messages we've been sending:

```
root@junade-test: ~/rabbitmq — ssh root@178.62.40.19      root@junade-test: ~/rabbitmq — ssh root@178.62.40.19

root@junade-test:~/rabbitmq# php recieve.php
Received: Hello world!
Received: Hello world!
Received: Hello world!
```

The RabbitMQ documentation uses the following diagram to describe the basic accepting and forwarding of messages:

Publish-Subscriber pattern

The Publish-Subscriber pattern (or Pub/Sub for short) is a design pattern whereby messages aren't directly sent from publisher to subscribers; instead, publishers push out the message without any knowledge.

In RabbitMQ, the *producer* never sends any messages directly to the queue. Quite often, the producer doesn't even know if the message will end up in a queue at all. Instead, the producer must send messages to an *exchange*. It receives messages from producers then pushes them out to queues.

The *consumer* is the application that will receive the messages.

The exchange must be told exactly how to handle a given message, and which queue(s) it should be appended to. These rules are defined by the *exchange type*.

The RabbitMQ documentation describes a Publish-Subscriber relationship (connecting the publisher, exchange, queue, and consumer) as follows:

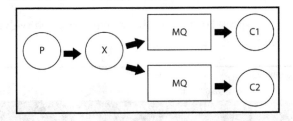

A *direct* exchange type delivers messages based on a routing key. It can be used both for one-to-one and one-to-many forms of routing, but it is best suited to a one-to-one relationship.

A *fanout* exchange type routes messages to all queues that are bound to it and the routing key is completely ignored. Effectively, you cannot differentiate between which workers messages will be distributed to based on the routing key.

A *topic* exchange type works by routing messages to one or many queues on the basis of a messaging routing queue and the pattern that was used to bind a queue to an exchange. This exchange has the potential to work well when are multiple consumers/applications that want to choose the type of messages they want to receive, usually in a many-to-many relationship.

The *headers* exchange type is commonly used to route on a set of attributes that are better expressed in message headers than the routing queue. Instead of using routing keys, the attributes to the route are based on the headers attribute.

In order to test a Pub/Sub queue, we will be using the following scripts. They are similar to the one in the example earlier, except I have modified them so that they use exchanges. Here is our `send.php` file:

```php
<?php

require_once(__DIR__ . '/vendor/autoload.php');
use PhpAmqpLib\Connection\AMQPStreamConnection;
use PhpAmqpLib\Message\AMQPMessage;

$connection = new AMQPStreamConnection('localhost', 5672, 'junade',
'insecurepassword');
$channel    = $connection->channel();

$channel->exchange_declare(
    'helloHello',    // exchange
    'fanout',        // exchange type
    false,           // passive
    false,           // durable
    false            // auto-delete
);

$msg = new AMQPMessage("Hello world!");

$channel->basic_publish(
    $msg,            // message
    'helloHello'     // exchange
);

$channel->close();
$connection->close();

echo "Sent hello world message." . PHP_EOL;
```

Here is our `receive.php` file. Like before, I have modified this script so that it also uses exchanges:

```php
<?php

require_once(__DIR__ . '/vendor/autoload.php');
use PhpAmqpLib\Connection\AMQPStreamConnection;
use PhpAmqpLib\Message\AMQPMessage;

$connection = new AMQPStreamConnection('localhost', 5672, 'junade',
'insecurepassword');
$channel    = $connection->channel();

$channel->exchange_declare(
  'helloHello',    // exchange
  'fanout',        // exchange type
  false,           // passive
  false,           // durable
  false            // auto-delete
);

$callback = function ($msg) {
  echo "Received: " . $msg->body . PHP_EOL;
};

list($queueName, ,) = $channel->queue_declare("", false, false, true,
false);

$channel->queue_bind($queueName, 'helloHello');

$channel->basic_consume($queueName, '', false, true, false, false,
$callback);

while (count($channel->callbacks)) {
  $channel->wait();
}

$channel->close();
$connection->close();
```

Now, let's test these scripts. We'll first need to have our `receive.php` script running, then we can send messages across using our `send.php` script.

First, let's trigger our `receive.php` script so that it starts running:

```
[root@junade-test:~/pubsub# php recieve.php
```

After this is complete we can then move on to sending messages by running our `send.php` script:

```
[root@junade-test:~/pubsub# php send.php
Sent hello world message.
root@junade-test:~/pubsub#
```

This will now populate our Terminal running `receive.php` with the following information:

Summary

In this chapter, we learned about Architectural patterns. Starting with MVC, we learned the benefits and challenges of using UI frameworks and discussed how we can decouple our UI from our business logic in a stricter fashion.

We then moved onto SOA and learned how this compared to microservices and where such architectures make sense, given the challenges distributed systems pose.

Finally, we did an in-depth tour of queuing systems, where they are appropriate, and how you can implement them in RabbitMQ.

In the next, and then the final chapter, we'll cover the best practice use conditions of Architectural patterns.

7
Refactoring

Throughout this book I have largely focused on using design patterns to address new code that you write; this is critical, it is vital that developers don't write the new legacy, improving your own code is vital before critiquing the code of others. Developers must first seek to understand how to code before they themselves may refactor code effectively.

This chapter shall be heavily based on *Refactoring: Improving the Design of Existing Code* by *Martin Fowler* et al alongside *Refactoring To Patterns* by *Joshua Kerievsky*. I would highly recommend reading these books if you are interested in learning more about this subject.

What is refactoring?

A key theme in refactoring code is addressing issues within the internal structure of code while not altering the external behavior of the program being refactored. In some cases, this can mean introducing internal structure where it previously wasn't intentional or thought about before.

Refactoring as a process improves the design of code after it is written. While design is a critical phase of the software engineering process, it is often disregarded (not least in PHP); in addition to this, maintaining the structure of code over the long-term requires a continued understanding of the design of software. If a developer takes up a project without understanding how it was originally designed, they may develop upon it in a very crude fashion.

In **Extreme Programming** (**XP**), a phrase known as *Refactor Mercilessly* is used, it is self-explanatory. In XP, refactoring is proposed as a mechanism to keep software design as simple as possible and to avoid needless complexity. As is stated in the rules of XP: *Make sure everything is expressed once and only once. In the end it takes less time to produce a system that is well groomed.*

A key tenet of refactoring is finding the software design as if it is something to be discovered instead of being created upfront. When developing a system, we can use development as a mechanism of finding a good design solution. By using refactoring, we are able to ensure that a system stays good as systems are developed, thus we are able to keep technical debt down.

Refactoring isn't always possible, you may occasionally encounter *black-box* systems which you cannot alter, indeed you may even need to encapsulate a system in order to rewrite it. There are, however, many cases in which we can simply refactor code to improve the design.

Test, test, and test again

There is no way around this, in order to refactor code, you need a solid set of tests. Refactoring code may well reduce the chances of introducing bugs, but changing the design of code introduces a significant amount of chances to introduce new bugs.

Unintended side-effects will occur during refactoring, where classes are tightly coupled, you may well find making a minor change to one function leading to a negative side-effect in a completely separate class.

Good refactoring effects require good tests. There is simply no way around this.

In addition to this, from a more political standpoint, some companies which have encountered the bad effects of repetitively bad refactoring efforts may become reluctant to refactor code; ensuring there are good tests in place allows the company to ensure a refactoring effort won't break functionality.

In this chapter I will demonstrate refactoring efforts which should be accompanied with testing efforts using unit tests, in the next (and final) chapter of this book, I will discuss behavioral tests (for use in BDD). Unit tests are the best mechanism developers have for testing a given unit of code; unit tests complement code structure, prove methods do what they should, and test interaction between units of code; in this sense, they are the best form of testing at the disposal of a developer in a refactoring effort. Behavioral tests however are there to test the behavior of code, thus are useful in order to demonstrate an application can successfully complete a given form of behavior.

Every seasoned developer will have memories of painful debugging tasks; sometimes long into the night. Let's think about how most developers work on a day-to-day basis. They don't code all the time, some of their time is spent around designing code while a considerable amount of time is spent debugging code they've already written. Having self-testing code can rapidly reduce this burden.

Test-Driven Development centers around a methodology of writing a test before writing functionality, indeed the code should match the test.

When testing classes, be sure to test the `public` interface of the class; indeed, PHPUnit will not allow you to test `private` or `protected` methods under ordinary usage.

Code smells

Code smells are essentially bits of bad practice that make your code needlessly harder to understand, bad code may be refactored away using the techniques expressed in this chapter. Code smells can usually violate somewhat fundamental software design principles and accordingly, can negatively impact design quality of the overall code.

Martin Fowler defined code smell by stating the following:

> *"a code smell is a surface indication that usually corresponds to a deeper problem in the system".*

At the start of this book we discussed the term *technical debt*, in this sense, code smells can contribute to *technical debt* as a whole.

Code smell may not necessarily constitute a bug, it won't stop the execution of a program, but it can aid the process of introducing bugs later on and make it harder to refactor code to an appropriate design.

Let's cover some fundamental code smells that you may encounter when dealing with legacy PHP projects.

We will address some code smells and how to address them in quite simplistic ways, but now let us consider some slightly more significant, recurring patterns and how these can be addressed by applying design patterns in order to simplify the maintenance of code going forward.

Here we will specifically talk about refactoring *to* patterns, in some cases, you may benefit from refactoring *from* patterns when it simplifies the design of the code. The recurring theme in this chapter surrounds how the design of code lives throughout the development life cycle of the code, it isn't merely discarded after an arbitrary design phase.

Patterns can be used to communicate intention, they can serve as the language between developers; this is why knowing and continuing to use a large body of patterns is vital throughout the career of a software engineer.

Many more of these approaches are available in the book *Refactoring To Patterns*, here I have handpicked the ones most appropriate to PHP developers.

Long methods and duplicated code

Duplicated code is a very common code smell. Developers will frequently copy and paste code instead of using an appropriate control structure for their application. If the same control structure is in more than one place, your code will benefit by merging the two structures into one.

If duplicated code is identical, you can use the extract method. So what is the extract method? In essence, the **extract method** is merely removing business logic that is vested in long functions into smaller functions.

Let's imagine a `dice` class, once the dice is rolled it will return a random number between 1 and 6 in Roman numerals.

The `Legacy` class can look like this:

```
class LegacyDice
{
  public function roll(): string
  {
    $rand = rand(1, 6);
    // Switch statement to convert a number between 1 and 6 to a Roman
Numeral.
    switch ($rand) {
      case 5:
        $randString = "V";
        break;
      case 6:
        $randString = "VI";
        break;
      default:
        $randString = str_repeat("I", $rand);
```

```
        break;
    }

    return $randString;
  }
}
```

Let's extract the method to convert a random number into a Roman numeral and put it into a separate function:

```
class Dice
{
  /**
   * Roll the dice.
   * @return string
   */
  public function roll(): string
  {
    $rand = rand(1, 6);

    return $this->numberToRomanNumeral($rand);
  }

  /**
   * Convert a number between 1 and 6 to a Roman Numeral.
   *
   * @param int $number
   *
   * @return string
   * @throws Exception
   */
  public function numberToRomanNumeral(int $number): string
  {
    if (($number < 1) || ($number > 6)) {
      throw new Exception('Number out of range.');
    }

    switch ($number) {
      case 5:
        $randString = "V";
        break;
      case 6:
        $randString = "VI";
        break;
      default:
        $randString = str_repeat("I", $number);
        break;
    }
```

```
    return $randString;
  }
}
```

There are merely two changes we have made to the original code block, we have separated out that function which performs Roman numeral conversion and put it in a separate function. We have replaced that inline comment with a DocBlock for the function itself.

This approach can be used for duplication, if it exists in more than one place (and is identical), we simply call a single function instead of having the code duplicated across multiple places.

If the code is in unrelated classes, see where it logically fits (in either of the classes or a separate class) and extract it there.

Earlier in this book, we have already discussed the need to keep functions small. This is absolutely vital for ensuring your code is readable in the long term.

I frequently see developers comment blocks of code within functions; instead, why not break out these methods into their own functions? Readable documentation may then be added through DocBlocks. Thus, the extract method we are using here to address duplicated code can have a much simpler use; breaking up long methods.

Solutions to various business problems are far easier shared when dealing with smaller methods.

Large class

Large classes often emerge as a violation of the Single Responsibility Principle. Does the class you are dealing with, at a given point in time, have only one reason to change? A class should only have responsibility over a single part of the functionality, furthermore, that class should entirely encapsulate that responsibility.

Dividing up the class into multiple classes by extracting methods which don't narrowly align to single responsibility is an easy and effective way to help mitigate this code smell.

Replacing complex logical statements and switch statements with polymorphism or the Strategy Pattern

Switch statements (or endlessly large if statements, for that matter) can largely be removed by using polymorphic behavior; I have described polymorphism in the early chapters of this book and it provides a far more elegant way of dealing with computational problems than using switch statements.

Suppose you were switching on a country code; US or GB, instead of switching in such a fashion, by using polymorphism you can run the same method.

Where polymorphic behavior is not possible (for example, where there isn't a common interface), in some cases you may even benefit by replacing type code with strategy; effectively you are able to consolidate the multiple switch statements into merely injecting a class into the constructor of a client which will handle the relation to the individual classes itself.

For example; let's suppose we have an Output interface, this interface is implemented by various other classes that contain a `load` method. This `load` method allows us to inject an array and we get back some data in the format we requested. These classes are incredibly crude implementations of that behavior:

```
interface Output
{
  public function load(array $data);
}

class Serial implements Output
{
  public function load(array $data)
  {
    return serialize($data);
  }
}

class JSON implements Output
{
  public function load(array $data)
  {
    return json_encode($data);
  }
}
```

```
class XML implements Output
{
  public function load(array $data)
  {
    return xmlrpc_encode($data);
  }
}
```

 At the time fo writing, PHP still deems the `xmlrpc_encode` function to be experimental, for this reason, I would advise against its use in production. It's just here purely for demonstration purposes (in order to keep the code short).

An incredibly crude implementation with a `switch` statement could be as follows:

```
$client = "JSON";

switch ($client) {
  case "Serial":
    $client = new Serial();
    break;
  case "JSON":
    $client = new JSON();
    break;
  case "XML":
    $client = new XML();
    break;
}

echo $client->load(array(1, 2));
```

But clearly we can do a lot by, instead, implementing a client that will allow us to inject an `Output` class into a `Client` and accordingly allow us to receive the output. Such a class may look like this:

```
class OutputClient
{
  private $output;

  public function __construct(Output $outputType)
  {
    $this->output = $outputType;
  }

  public function loadOutput(array $data)
  {
    return $this->output->load($data);
```

```
    }
}
```

We can now utilize this client in a very simple fashion:

```
$client = new OutputClient(new JSON());
echo $client->loadOutput(array(1, 2));
```

Duplicating code following a single control structure

I won't reiterate here how the Template design pattern works, but what I want to explain is that it can be used to help eliminate duplicate code.

The Template design pattern I demonstrated earlier in this book allowed us to effectively abstract away the structure of a program, we then just populated the methods specific to an implementation. This can help us reduce code duplication by avoiding repeating a single control structure over and over.

Long Parameter List and primitive obsession

Primitive obsession is where developers over-use primitive data types instead of using objects.

PHP supports eight primitive types; this group can further be subdivided into scalar types, compound types, and special types.

Scalar types are the data types which hold a single value. You can recognize them if you ask yourself "can this value be on a scale?" A number can be on a scale from X to Y and a Boolean could be on a scale from false to true. Here are some examples of scalar types:

- Boolean
- Integer
- Float
- String

Compound types consist of a set of scalar values:

- Array
- Object

Special types are as follows:

- Resource (references an external resource)
- NULL

Suppose we have a simple `Salary` calculator class, it takes an employee's base salary, commission rate, and pension rate; after this data is sent, the `calculate` method can be used to input the amount of sales they have made to calculate their total salary:

```
class Salary
{
  private $baseSalary;
  private $commission = 0;
  private $pension = 0;

  public function __construct(float $baseSalary, float $commission, float
$pension)
  {
    $this->baseSalary = $baseSalary;
    $this->commission = $commission;
    $this->pension    = $pension;
  }

  public function calculate(float $sales): float
  {
    $base       = $this->baseSalary;
    $commission = $this->commission * $sales;
    $deducation = $base * $this->pension;

    return $commission + $base - $deducation;
  }
}
```

Note how long that constructor is. Yes, we could use the Builder pattern to create an object which we can then inject into the constructor, but in this case, we are able to specifically abstract away the complicated information. In this case, if we were to move the employee information to a separate class we could ensure better compliance with the Single Responsibility Principle.

The first step is to separate out the responsibilities of the class so that we can separate the responsibilities of the class:

```php
class Employee
{
  private $name;
  private $baseSalary;
  private $commission = 0;
  private $pension = 0;

  public function __construct(string $name, float $baseSalary)
  {
    $this->name       = $name;
    $this->baseSalary = $baseSalary;
  }

  public function getBaseSalary(): float
  {
    return $this->baseSalary;
  }

  public function setCommission(float $percentage)
  {
    $this->commission = $percentage;
  }

  public function getCommission(): float
  {
    return $this->commission;
  }

  public function setPension(float $rate)
  {
    $this->pension = $rate;
  }

  public function getPension(): float
  {
    return $this->commission;
  }
}
```

From this point, we can simplify the constructor of our `Salary` class so that it only needs to input the `Employee` object for us to be able to use the class:

```php
class Salary
{
  private $employee;
```

```php
    public function __construct(Employee $employee)
    {
      $this->employee = $employee;
    }

    public function calculate(float $sales): float
    {
      $base       = $this->employee->getBaseSalary();
      $commission = $this->employee->getCommission() * $sales;
      $deducation = $base * $this->employee->getPension();

      return $commission + $base - $deducation;
    }
}
```

Indecent exposure

Let's suppose we have a Human class as follows:

```php
class Human
{
  public $name;
  public $dateOfBirth;
  public $height;
  public $weight;
}
```

We are able to set the values as we please, with no validation and no unified way of getting information. What's so wrong with this? Well, in object orientation, the principle of encapsulation is vital; we hide data. In other words, our data should never be made visible without the owning object knowing it.

Instead, we substitute all the public data variables with private ones. In addition to this we add appropriate methods to get and set the data:

```php
class Human
{
  private $name;
  private $dateOfBirth;
  private $height;
  private $weight;

  public function __construct(string $name, double $dateOfBirth)
  {
    $this->name        = $name;
    $this->dateOfBirth = $dateOfBirth;
```

```
    }

    public function setWeight(double $weight)
    {
      $this->weight = $weight;
    }

    public function getWeight(): double
    {
      return $this->weight;
    }

    public function setHeight(double $height)
    {
      $this->height = $height;
    }

    public function getHeight(): double
    {
      return $this->height;
    }
}
```

Be sure to ensure that setters and getters are logical and are not there merely because a class property exists. After this is complete you will need to go through your application and substitute any direct access to variables so that they go through the appropriate methods first.

This has, however, now exposed another code smell; feature envy.

Feature envy

Loosely, **feature envy** is where we don't get an object to do calculation of its own properties and instead offset that to another class.

So in the previous example we had our own `Salary` calculator class, as follows:

```
class Salary
{
  private $employee;

  public function __construct(Employee $employee)
  {
    $this->employee = $employee;
  }
```

```php
  public function calculate(float $sales): float
  {
    $base       = $this->employee->getBaseSalary();
    $commission = $this->employee->getCommission() * $sales;
    $deducation = $base * $this->employee->getPension();

    return $commission + $base - $deducation;
  }
}
```

Instead let's take a look at implementing this function into the Employee class itself, as a result we can also disregard the unnecessary getters and keep our properties rightfully internalized:

```php
class Employee
{
  private $name;
  private $baseSalary;
  private $commission = 0;
  private $pension = 0;

  public function __construct(string $name, float $baseSalary)
  {
    $this->name       = $name;
    $this->baseSalary = $baseSalary;
  }

  public function setCommission(float $percentage)
  {
    $this->commission = $percentage;
  }

  public function setPension(float $rate)
  {
    $this->pension = $rate;
  }

  public function calculate(float $sales): float
  {
    $base       = $this->baseSalary;
    $commission = $this->commission * $sales;
    $deducation = $base * $this->pension;

    return $commission + $base - $deducation;
  }
}
```

Inappropriate intimacy

This may frequently occur with inheritance; Martin Fowler elegantly puts it as follows:

> *"Subclasses are always going to know more about their parents than their parents would like them to know."*

More generally; when a field is used more in another class than the class itself, we can use the move field method to create a field in a new class, then redirect users of that field to the new class.

We can combine this with the move method, whereby we place a function in the class that uses it most and remove it from the original class, if that isn't possible we can get away with simply referencing the function in the new class.

Deeply nested statements

Nested if statements are messy and ugly. This causes spaghetti logic that is difficult to follow; instead use inline function calls.

Starting from the inner-most code block, seek to extract that code into its own function where it can live happily. In `Chapter 1`, *Why "Good PHP Developer" Isn't an Oxymoron* we discussed how this can be achieved with an example, but if you're refactoring frequently you might want to consider investing in a tool which can help you with this.

Here's a tip for the PHPStorm users among us: there is a lovely little option within the Refactor menu that can do this for you automatically. Simply highlight the code block you wish to extract, go to **Refactor** in the menu bar then click **Extract>Method**. A dialog will then pop up allowing you to configure how you want the refactoring to run:

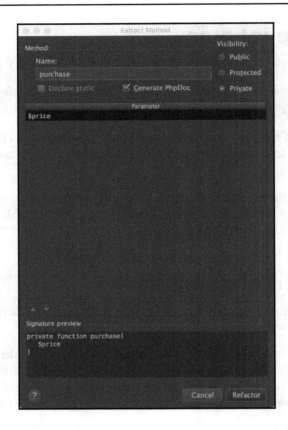

Remove assignments to parameters

Try to avoid setting a parameter in the body of a function:

```php
class Before
{
  function deductTax(float $salary, float $rate): float
  {
    $salary = $salary * $rate;

    return $salary;
  }
}
```

This can be done correctly by setting an internal parameter instead:

```
class After
{
  function deductTax(float $salary, float $rate): float
  {
    $netSalary = $salary * $rate;

    return $netSalary;
  }
}
```

By doing such behavior we are able to easily identify and extract repetitive code going forward, in addition to this it allows easier code replacement when maintaining this code later.

This is a simple tweak which allows us to identify what particular parameters in our code are doing.

Comments

Comments aren't a code smell per-se, in many cases, comments are hugely beneficial. As Martin Fowler states:

> *"In our olfactory analogy, comments aren't a bad smell; indeed they are a sweet smell."*

However, Fowler goes on to demonstrate how comments may be used as the deodorant to hide code smells. When you find yourself commenting code blocks within functions you can find a good opportunity to use the extract method.

If a comment is hiding a bad smell, refactor the smell away and you will soon find the original comment being superfluous. This isn't an excuse not to DocBlock your function or needlessly go on a hunt for code comments, but it is important to remember that specific comments may become useless when you refactor a design to be far more simplistic.

Encapsulating Composite with Builder

As discussed earlier in this book, the Builder design pattern can work by us taking a long set of arguments and turning them into a single object which we can then throw into the constructor of another class.

For example, we have a class called `APIBuilder`, this builder class can then itself be instantiated with the API key and secret of the API, but once it's instantiated as an object, we can simply pass the entire object into the constructor of another class.

So far, so good; but we can use this Builder pattern to encapsulate the Composite pattern. We effectively just create a Builder to create our items. By doing this we have greater control with a single class offering us an opportunity to navigate and alter the entire tree structure of the Composite family.

Replacing hard-coded notifications with Observer

Hard-coded notifications are usually where two classes are tightly coupled together in order for one to be able to notify the other. Instead, by using the `SplObserver` and `SplSubject` interfaces, the Observer can update the subject using a far more pluggable. After implementing an `update` method in the Observer, the subject merely needs to implement the `Subject` interface:

```
SplSubject {
    /* Methods */
    abstract public void attach ( SplObserver $observer )
    abstract public void detach ( SplObserver $observer )
    abstract public void notify ( void )
}
```

The resulting architecture is a far more pluggable notification system which is not tightly coupled.

Replacing one/many distinctions with Composite

Where we have separate logic for handing individuals to groups, we can consolidate these using the Composite pattern. This is a pattern we have covered earlier this book; in order to consolidate to this pattern, a developer needs only alter their code so that one class can handle both forms of data.

In order to achieve this, we must first ensure both the distinctions implement the same interface.

When I initially demonstrated this pattern, I wrote about how this pattern can be used to address treating a single song and a playlist as one. Suppose our `Music` interface is purely the following:

```
interface Music
{
  public function play();
}
```

The critical task is just ensuring that this interface is abided by for both the one and the many distinctions. Both your `Song` class and your `Playlist` class must implement the `Music` interface. This is fundamentally what allows us to treat both with the behavior.

Separate versions with Adapters

I won't dwell on Adapters for long due to how thoroughly I covered them earlier in this book, but I just want you to consider that they can be used for supporting different versions of APIs.

Be sure not to wrap code together in the same class for multiple API versions instead, you can abstract these differences from version-to-version to an Adapter. When using this approach, I would urge you to initially attempt to use an encapsulation approach rather than an inheritance-based approach as this will provide greater freedom going forward.

What do I tell my manager?

Refactoring and then adding functionality can often be faster than simply adding the functionality while adding value to the existing code base. Many good managers, who properly understand software and how it is developed will understand this.

Of course there are managers who are clueless about what software actually is, they are often driven solely by deadlines and may be reluctant to learn more about their subject field. I am talking about the horror story developers I have mentioned earlier in this book. Sometimes, *Scrum Masters* are also guilty of this, due to the fact they may not be able to relate to the entire software development life cycle.

As Martin Fowler himself put it:

> *"Of course, many people say they are driven by quality but are more driven by schedule. In these cases I give my more controversial advice: Don't tell!"*

Managers who don't properly understand technical processes may be intent on delivering on the basis of how rapidly software can be produced; refactoring can prove to be the most rapid way of helping produce software. It provides an efficient and thorough way to get up to speed with a project and allows us to smooth the process of injecting in new functionality.

We will discuss management and how projects can be effectively managed in the next chapter of this book.

Summary

In this chapter, we've discussed some methods of refactoring code to ensure the design is always of a good quality. By refactoring code, we can gain a greater understanding of our code base and future-proof it for the additional functionality that we add to the software.

Simplification and breaking down the problems you face are two of the best fundamental tools you can use when refactoring code.

If you are using a CI environment, having PHP Mess Detector (PHPMD) running on that environment can also help you code better.

In the next chapter, I will discuss how we can use design patterns appropriately, starting off with a quick lesson on developing APIs in the context of a network.

8
How to Write Better Code

This is the final chapter in this book. We've discussed a lot of patterns, but in this final chapter I want us to discuss how these patterns can be applied.

I want us here to talk about the bigger picture about how our code fits together, and what the key takeaways are for us to write great code.

In addition to this, I would like to discuss where patterns are suited to our application in the development phase.

In this chapter, we'll cover the following points:

- The nature of an HTTP request
- RESTful API design
- Keep It Simple, Stupid
- Software development life cycle and engineering practices
- The importance of testing
- A light introduction to BDD

Nature of a HTTP request

Many developers find HTTP requests are abstracted away from them; indeed, many PHP developers will never need to understand how an HTTP request actually works under the hood.

PHP developers often work with HTTP networks when developing. Indeed, PHP contains some core functions that are great when working with HTTP communication.

Let's take a look at an HTTP request at a high-level using a tool called **curl**. The curl is essentially a command-line tool that allows us to simulate network requests. It allows you to simulate the transfer of data using various protocols.

 The name of *cURL* originally stood for *see URL*.

The curl projects produce both the `libcurl` and `curl` command line tool. Libcurl is a library that PHP supports, allowing you to connect and communicate over a list of protocols in PHP, providing your installation has it installed.

In this case, however, we will be using the command-line tool to simulate requests.

Let's start off by making a simple `curl` request to a given website, as follows:

```
curl https://junade.com
```

Depending on the site you query in the command you will notice that the Terminal output is blank:

```
                          junade — -bash — 80×24
Last login: Sun Jul 10 19:05:55 on ttys005
[Junades-MacBook-Pro-2:~ junade$ curl http://junade.com                      ]
Junades-MacBook-Pro-2:~ junade$ 
```

What's going on here? In order to find out, we need to dig a little further.

You can use the `-v` argument in the `curl` command so we see a verbose output of what's going on:

```
curl -v ht
tp://junade.com
```

This output of this is substantially different:

```
                            ⬆ junade — -bash — 80×24
Last login: Sun Jul 10 19:20:30 on ttys004
Junades-MacBook-Pro-2:~ junade$ curl -v http://junade.com
* Rebuilt URL to: http://junade.com/
*   Trying 2400:cb00:2048:1::6810:f005...
* Connected to junade.com (::1) port 80 (#0)
> GET / HTTP/1.1
> Host: junade.com
> User-Agent: curl/7.43.0
> Accept: */*
>
< HTTP/1.1 301 Moved Permanently
< Date: Sun, 10 Jul 2016 18:23:22 GMT
< Transfer-Encoding: chunked
< Connection: keep-alive
< Set-Cookie: __cfduid=d45c9e013b12286fe4e443702f3ec15f31468175002; expires=Mon,
  10-Jul-17 18:23:22 GMT; path=/; domain=.junade.com; HttpOnly
< Location: https://junade.com/
< Server: cloudflare-nginx
< CF-RAY: 2c060be42065346a-LHR
<
* Connection #0 to host junade.com left intact
Junades-MacBook-Pro-2:~ junade$ ▯
```

With this output we can see the headers that are sent and the headers that are received.

The block starting with asterisks * indicates the connection being established. We can see how curl has rebuilt the URL so it is correct (containing a forward slash at the end), then resolved the IP address of the server (in my case, an IPv6 address), and then finally established the connection to the web server:

```
* Rebuilt URL to: http://junade.com/
*   Trying 2400:cb00:2048:1::6810:f005...
* Connected to junade.com (::1) port 80 (#0)
```

The hostname is turned into an IP address by querying the DNS server; we'll go into more detail about this later on. But at this point, it is important to remember that, after this point, the connection to the server is established using an IP address.

If we were to get rid of the forward slash at the end, we can actually see that in the first line, rebuilding the URL will disappear, as it will already be in the correct format before we even make the request:

```
Last login: Sun Jul 10 19:23:14 on ttys004
[Junades-MacBook-Pro-2:~ junade$ curl -v http://junade.com/
*    Trying 2400:cb00:2048:1::6810:f135...
* Connected to junade.com (::1) port 80 (#0)
> GET / HTTP/1.1
> Host: junade.com
> User-Agent: curl/7.43.0
> Accept: */*
>
< HTTP/1.1 301 Moved Permanently
< Date: Sun, 10 Jul 2016 18:30:19 GMT
< Transfer-Encoding: chunked
< Connection: keep-alive
< Set-Cookie: __cfduid=de4b48939edfd55891451f76b054db8411468175419; expires=Mon,
  10-Jul-17 18:30:19 GMT; path=/; domain=.junade.com; HttpOnly
< Location: https://junade.com/
< Server: cloudflare-nginx
< CF-RAY: 2c061615f4f83470-LHR
<
* Connection #0 to host junade.com left intact
Junades-MacBook-Pro-2:~ junade$ 
```

Next let's look at the succeeding lines the asterisks. We see the outbound headers in the greater than signs >.

These headers look like this:

```
> GET / HTTP/1.1
> Host: junade.com
> User-Agent: curl/7.43.0
> Accept: */*
>
```

So the first message we see is the request method GET, followed by the endpoint / and the protocol HTTP/1.1.

Next, we see the Host header, which tells us the domain name of the server and can also contain the TCP port number on which the server is listening, but this is often amended if the port is standard for the service requested. Why is this needed, though? Suppose a server contains many VirtualHosts; this is what actually allows the server to determine between VirtualHosts using the header. VirtualHosting essentially allows a server to host more than one domain name. In order to do this, we need this header; when a server sees a HTTP request coming in they won't see the header.

Remember when I said a connection is established using an IP address? This `Host` header is what allows us to send through that hostname variable indicating what an IP address is.

Next, we see the `User-Agent` header, indicating what browser the client is using; our `User-Agent` header in this request indicates we are sending our HTTP request using curl command. Remember not to trust any HTTP headers from the client, as they can be manipulated to contain whatever data a malicious adversary wants to put into them. They can contain everything from a fake browser identifier to a SQL injection.

Finally, the `Accept` header indicates the `Content-Type` headers that are acceptable for the response. Here, we see a wildcard acceptance, indicating we are happy to receive whatever the server is sending us. In other cases, we can use `Accept: text/plain` to indicate that we want to see plaintext, or `Accept:application/json` for JSON. We can even specify if we want to receive a PNG image by using `Accept: image/png`.

There are various parameters that can also be sent to over an `Accept` header; for example, we can request HTML using a UTF-8 charset with Accept: `text/html; charset=UTF-8`.

At a basic level, the syntax that is permissible in this header looks like this:

```
top-level type name / subtype name [ ; parameters ]
```

The server can indicate the content type being returned to the user using a `Content-Type` header in the response. So the server can send a header back to the end user as follows:

```
Content-Type: text/html; charset=utf-8
```

Moving onto the topic of the response, let's take a look at the response. These are prefixed with <:

```
< HTTP/1.1 301 Moved Permanently
< Date: Sun, 10 Jul 2016 18:23:22 GMT
< Transfer-Encoding: chunked
< Connection: keep-alive
< Set-Cookie: __cfduid=d45c9e013b12286fe4e443702f3ec15f31468175002;
expires=Mon, 10-Jul-17 18:23:22 GMT; path=/; domain=.junade.com; HttpOnly
< Location: https://junade.com/
< Server: cloudflare-nginx
< CF-RAY: 2c060be42065346a-LHR
<
```

So the first thing we get in the response indicating the format and the status code. HTTP/1.1 indicates that we are receiving a `HTTP/1.1` response, and a `301 Moved Permanently` message indicates a permanent redirect. Accordingly, we also receive a `Location:` `https://junade.com/` header, which tells us where to go next.

The `Server` header indicates the signature of the web server that is supplying our request. It could be Apache or Nginx; in this case, it's the modified version of Nginx that CloudFlare use for their network.

The Set-Cookie header is used to indicate what cookies the browser should set; the standard for this is in a document known as RFC 6265.

RFC stands for **Request for Comments**; there are a number of types of RFC. Standards Track RFCs are those intending to become Internet Standards (STDs), whereas Informational RFCs can be anything. There are a number of other types of RFC, such as Experimental, Best Current Practice, Historic, and even an Unknown RFC type for those where the status is unclear if they were to be published today.

The `Transfer-Encoding` header indicates the encoding used to transfer the entity to the user, which could be anything from chunked even to something such as gzip, which is a compressed entity.

Interestingly, the `HTTP/2` protocol that was published in RFC 7540 in May 2015 actually allows header compression. Nowadays, we send more in header data than was originally transmitted when the `HTTP/1` protocol was created (the original `HTTP` protocol didn't even contain a `Host` header!).

The `Connection` header provides control options for the connection. It allows the sender to specify the options that are desired for the current connection. Finally, the `Date` header indicates the date and time when the message was sent.

Consider this: can an HTTP request/response contain more than one of the same header of the name?

Yes, this is particularly useful in some headers, such as the `Link` header. This header is used to perform `HTTP/2` Server Push; Server Push allows the server to push requests to the client before they are requested. One asset can be specified per header; therefore, multiple headers are needed to push multiple assets.

This is something we can do in PHP. Take the following `header` function call in PHP:

```
header("Link: <{$uri}>; rel=preload; as=image", false);
```

While the first argument is the string of the actual header we're sending, the second argument (`false`) states that we don't want to replace a previous header of the same, instead we want to send this one as well but not replace it. By setting this flag to `true` we instead state that we want to override the previous header; this is the default option if the flag isn't specified at all.

Finally, when the request is closed you will see a final asterisk indicating the connection was closed:

```
* Connection #0 to host junade.com left intact
```

Typically, this will become below the body if there is one. In this request, there wasn't one as it was merely a redirect.

I now make a `curl` request to where that `Location` header is pointing using the following command:

curl -v https://junade.com/

You will now notice that the connection close message came after the end of the HTML body:

```
⟰ junade — -bash — 80×24
.009-0.423C14.976,4.29,15.531,3.714,15.969,3.058z"/></svg>
</span><span class="username">IcyApril</span></a>
</li>
</ul>
</div>
<div class="footer-col footer-col-3">
<p>Software Engineer, interested in software design and recovering from PHP, for
mally worked in IoT and road raffic data analysis. Interested in constitutional
law and politics. Nowadays, Community Manager at CloudFlare.</p>
</div>
</div>
</div>
</footer>
<script type="text/javascript">/* <![CDATA[ */(function(d,s,a,i,j,r,l,m,t){try{l
=d.getElementsByTagName('a');t=d.createElement('textarea');for(i=0;l.length-i;i+
+){try{a=l[i].href;s=a.indexOf('/cdn-cgi/l/email-protection');m=a.length;if(a&&s
>-1&&m>28){j=28+s;s='';if(j<m){r='0x'+a.substr(j,2)|0;for(j+=2;j<m&&a.charAt(j)!
='X';j+=2)s+='%'+('0'+('0x'+a.substr(j,2)^r).toString(16)).slice(-2);j++;s=decod
eURIComponent(s)+a.substr(j,m-j)}t.innerHTML=s.replace(/</g,'&lt;').replace(/>/g
,'&gt;');l[i].href='mailto:'+t.value}}catch(e){}}catch(e){}})(document);/* ]]>
*/</script></body>
</html>
* Connection #0 to host junade.com left intact
Junades-MacBook-Pro-2:~ junade$ 
```

Let's now try exploring a few HTTP methods. In REST APIs you will frequently use GET, POST, PUT, and DELETE; but first we'll start by exploring two others, HEAD and OPTIONS.

An `HTTP OPTIONS` request details which requests methods you can use on a given endpoint. It provides information about which communication options are available to that particular endpoint.

Let me demonstrate this. I'm going to be using a service called `HTTPBin`, which allows me to make requests to over curl to get some responses back from a real server.

Here's an `OPTIONS` request I'm making using curl:

```
curl -v -X OPTIONS https://httpbin.org/get
```

The `-X` option allows us to specify a particular HTTP request type instead of just defaulting to curl.

Let's see what this looks like once executed:

```
Junades-MacBook-Pro-2:~ junade$ curl -v -X OPTIONS https://httpbin.org/get
*   Trying 54.175.219.8...
* Connected to httpbin.org (54.175.219.8) port 443 (#0)
* TLS 1.2 connection using TLS_ECDHE_RSA_WITH_AES_256_GCM_SHA384
* Server certificate: *.httpbin.org
* Server certificate: COMODO RSA Domain Validation Secure Server CA
* Server certificate: COMODO RSA Certification Authority
* Server certificate: AddTrust External CA Root
> OPTIONS /get HTTP/1.1
> Host: httpbin.org
> User-Agent: curl/7.43.0
> Accept: */*
>
< HTTP/1.1 200 OK
< Server: nginx
< Date: Sun, 10 Jul 2016 20:26:11 GMT
< Content-Type: text/html; charset=utf-8
< Content-Length: 0
< Connection: keep-alive
< Allow: HEAD, OPTIONS, GET
< Access-Control-Allow-Origin: *
< Access-Control-Allow-Credentials: true
< Access-Control-Allow-Methods: GET, POST, PUT, DELETE, PATCH, OPTIONS
< Access-Control-Max-Age: 3600
<
* Connection #0 to host httpbin.org left intact
Junades-MacBook-Pro-2:~ junade$ 
```

Firstly, you'll notice that, given the request is over HTTP, you will see some extra information in the asterisk; this information contains the TLS certificate information that is used to encrypt the connection.

Take a look at the following line:

```
TLS 1.2 connection using TLS_ECDHE_RSA_WITH_AES_256_GCM_SHA384
```

`TLS 1.2` indicates the version of transport layer security we're dealing with; the second part, which states `TLS_ECDHE_RSA_WITH_AES_256_GCM_SHA384`, indicates the cipher suite for the connection.

The cipher suite starts by detailing that we're dealing with `TLS`. `ECDHE_RSA` indicates that the key exchange is done using elliptic curve Diffie-Hellman. The key exchange essentially allows the encryption keys to be transmitted securely. By using elliptic curve cryptography, a particular key can be shared, which can then be used to encrypt data later on. `ECDHE_RSA` means that we use elliptic curve Diffie-Hellman to share a key based on an RSA key that the server has gotten. There are a number of other key exchange algorithms; for example, `ECDH_ECDSA` uses Fixed ECDH with ECDSA-signed certificates.

The access-control prefixed headers are used for a mechanism called CORS, which essentially allows JavaScript to make cross-origin API requests; let's not worry about this here.

The header we do need to worry about with an `OPTIONS` request is the `Allow` header. This details what request methods we're allowed to submit back to that particular endpoint.

Therefore, this is the request we get when we query the `/get` endpoint:

```
< Allow: HEAD, OPTIONS, GET
```

Note that the endpoint I use here uses the `/get` endpoint. Instead, let's make another `OPTIONS` request to the `/post` endpoint using the following `curl` request:

```
curl -v -X OPTIONS https://httpbin.org/post
```

This is the response we get back:

```
● ● ●                    ⌂ junade — -bash — 80×29
[Junades-MacBook-Pro-2:~ junade$ curl -v -X OPTIONS https://httpbin.org/post ]
*    Trying 23.22.14.18...
* Connected to httpbin.org (23.22.14.18) port 443 (#0)
* TLS 1.2 connection using TLS_ECDHE_RSA_WITH_AES_256_GCM_SHA384
* Server certificate: *.httpbin.org
* Server certificate: COMODO RSA Domain Validation Secure Server CA
* Server certificate: COMODO RSA Certification Authority
* Server certificate: AddTrust External CA Root
> OPTIONS /post HTTP/1.1
> Host: httpbin.org
> User-Agent: curl/7.43.0
> Accept: */*
>
< HTTP/1.1 200 OK
< Server: nginx
< Date: Sun, 10 Jul 2016 20:49:32 GMT
< Content-Type: text/html; charset=utf-8
< Content-Length: 0
< Connection: keep-alive
< Allow: POST, OPTIONS
< Access-Control-Allow-Origin: *
< Access-Control-Allow-Credentials: true
< Access-Control-Allow-Methods: GET, POST, PUT, DELETE, PATCH, OPTIONS
< Access-Control-Max-Age: 3600
<
* Connection #0 to host httpbin.org left intact
Junades-MacBook-Pro-2:~ junade$ ▯
```

You'll notice that the `Allow` header now contains `POST` and `OPTIONS`. Also note that the HEAD option has gone.

You'll soon find out that a HEAD request is very similar to a GET request except without a message body. It merely returns the headers of a HTTP request but not the body of a request. Thus, it allows you to get the meta information about an entity without needing to get the complete response.

Let's make a HEAD request to a /get endpoint:

```
curl -I -X HEAD https://httpbin.org/get
```

Instead of using the -v (verbose) option in this request, I'm using the -I option, which will merely get the HTTP header. This is well suited to making an HTTP request using the HEAD option:

```
                          junade — -bash — 80×24
Last login: Sun Jul 10 21:32:41 on ttys007
Junades-MacBook-Pro-2:~ junade$ curl -I -X HEAD https://httpbin.org/get
HTTP/1.1 200 OK
Server: nginx
Date: Sun, 10 Jul 2016 20:56:17 GMT
Content-Type: application/json
Content-Length: 187
Connection: keep-alive
Access-Control-Allow-Origin: *
Access-Control-Allow-Credentials: true

Junades-MacBook-Pro-2:~ junade$ 
```

As you can see, we get the type of the response in the Content-Type header. Alongside this, you'll get the length of the request in the Content-Length header. The length is measured in octets (8 bits); you might think that is is the same as a byte, but a byte is not necessarily 8 bits on all architectures.

There are a number of other headers that can be sent to express meta information. This may include standard headers or non-standard headers to express other information that you can't express in standardized RFC-backed headers.

HTTP ETags (entity tags) are a mechanism that provide cache validation. You can use them in the context of RESTful APIs for optimistic concurrency control; this basically allows multiple requests to complete without needing to interfere with each other. This is quite an advanced API concept, so I won't go into too much detail here.

Note that in both our HTTP HEAD and OPTIONS request we both got 200 OK header messages. A 200 status code indicates a successful HTTP request.

There are many different types of status code. They are categorized as follows:

- **1xx messages**: Informational
- **2xx messages**: Success
- **3xx messages**: Redirect
- **4xx messages**: Client Error

- **5xx messages**: Server Error

An informational header could be a `101` response, which indicates the client is switching protocols and the server has agreed to do so. You probably won't encounter informational header messages if you're developing RESTful APIs; these are most likely things that will be sent by the web server, which is abstracted away from you as a developer.

Correct use of the other HTTP status codes is vital for correct development of a API, particularly one that is RESTful.

Success status codes aren't just limited to a `200 OK` message; 201 Created indicates a request has been fulfilled that has created a new resource. This is particularly useful when a `PUT` request is made to create a new resource or using `POST` to create a subsidiary resource. `202 Accepted` indicates a request has been accepted for processing but processing has not been completed, which is useful in a distributed system. `204 No Content` indicates the server has processed the request and is not returning any information; a `205 Reset Content` header does the same but asks the requester to reset their document view. These are just a few 200's messages; there are obviously many more.

Redirection messages include `301 Moved Permanently`, which we showed in our first `curl` example, whereas `302 Found` can be used for more temporary redirects. Again, there are other message codes.

Client error codes include the infamous `404 Not Found` message when a resource cannot be found. Alongside this, we have `401 Unauthorized` when authentication is required but not provided, `403 Forbidden` is where a server refuses to respond to a request at all (for example, incorrect permissions). `405 Method Not Allowed` allows us to deny requests on the basis of them being submitted using an invalid request method, which is, again, very useful for RESTful APIs. `405 Not Acceptable` is a response where the server cannot generate a response in accordance with the `Accept` header sent to it. Again, there are numerous other 4xx HTTP codes.

 HTTP code 451 indicates a request is unavailable for legal reasons. The code chosen after *Fahrenheit 451*, a novel named after the author claimed 451 Fahrenheit was the auto-ignition temperature of paper.

Finally, `Server Errors` allow the server to indicate they failed to fulfill a request that was apparently valid. These messages included the `500 Internal Server Error`, which is a generic error message given when an unexpected condition is encountered.

Let's now look at making a GET request. The curl, by default will make a GET request if we don't specify any data to send or a particular method:

```
curl -v https://httpbin.org/get
```

We can also specify that we want a GET request:

```
curl -v -X GET https://httpbin.org/get
```

The output of this is as follows:

```
                         ⬆ junade — -bash — 80×34
Junades-MacBook-Pro-2:~ junade$ curl -v -X GET https://httpbin.org/get
*   Trying 23.22.14.18...
* Connected to httpbin.org (23.22.14.18) port 443 (#0)
* TLS 1.2 connection using TLS_ECDHE_RSA_WITH_AES_256_GCM_SHA384
* Server certificate: *.httpbin.org
* Server certificate: COMODO RSA Domain Validation Secure Server CA
* Server certificate: COMODO RSA Certification Authority
* Server certificate: AddTrust External CA Root
> GET /get HTTP/1.1
> Host: httpbin.org
> User-Agent: curl/7.43.0
> Accept: */*
>
< HTTP/1.1 200 OK
< Server: nginx
< Date: Sun, 10 Jul 2016 21:48:53 GMT
< Content-Type: application/json
< Content-Length: 187
< Connection: keep-alive
< Access-Control-Allow-Origin: *
< Access-Control-Allow-Credentials: true
<
{
  "args": {},
  "headers": {
    "Accept": "*/*",
    "Host": "httpbin.org",
    "User-Agent": "curl/7.43.0"
  },
  "origin": "185.122.0.240",
  "url": "https://httpbin.org/get"
}
* Connection #0 to host httpbin.org left intact
Junades-MacBook-Pro-2:~ junade$ ▯
```

Here, you can see we get the same headers as we did in the HEAD request, with the addition of a body; some JSON data of whatever resource we're trying to access.

There we get a 200 Success message, but let's make a HTTP request to an endpoint that doesn't exist so we can trigger a 404 message:

```
                            junade — -bash — 80×29
Junades-MacBook-Pro-2:~ junade$ curl -v -X GET https://httpbin.org/doesntexist
*   Trying 23.22.14.18...
* Connected to httpbin.org (23.22.14.18) port 443 (#0)
* TLS 1.2 connection using TLS_ECDHE_RSA_WITH_AES_256_GCM_SHA384
* Server certificate: *.httpbin.org
* Server certificate: COMODO RSA Domain Validation Secure Server CA
* Server certificate: COMODO RSA Certification Authority
* Server certificate: AddTrust External CA Root
> GET /doesntexist HTTP/1.1
> Host: httpbin.org
> User-Agent: curl/7.43.0
> Accept: */*
>
< HTTP/1.1 404 NOT FOUND
< Server: nginx
< Date: Sun, 10 Jul 2016 21:50:15 GMT
< Content-Type: text/html
< Content-Length: 233
< Connection: keep-alive
< Access-Control-Allow-Origin: *
< Access-Control-Allow-Credentials: true
<
<!DOCTYPE HTML PUBLIC "-//W3C//DTD HTML 3.2 Final//EN">
<title>404 Not Found</title>
<h1>Not Found</h1>
<p>The requested URL was not found on the server.  If you entered the URL manual
ly please check your spelling and try again.</p>
* Connection #0 to host httpbin.org left intact
Junades-MacBook-Pro-2:~ junade$
```

As you can see, we get a header stating 404 NOT FOUND instead of our usual 200 OK message.

`HTTP 404` responses can also come without a body:

```
● ● ●                      ⇧ junade — -bash — 80×24
Junades-MacBook-Pro-2:~ junade$ curl -v -X GET https://httpbin.org/status/404
*   Trying 54.175.219.8...
* Connected to httpbin.org (54.175.219.8) port 443 (#0)
* TLS 1.2 connection using TLS_ECDHE_RSA_WITH_AES_256_GCM_SHA384
* Server certificate: *.httpbin.org
* Server certificate: COMODO RSA Domain Validation Secure Server CA
* Server certificate: COMODO RSA Certification Authority
* Server certificate: AddTrust External CA Root
> GET /status/404 HTTP/1.1
> Host: httpbin.org
> User-Agent: curl/7.43.0
> Accept: */*
>
< HTTP/1.1 404 NOT FOUND
< Server: nginx
< Date: Sun, 10 Jul 2016 21:52:49 GMT
< Content-Type: text/html; charset=utf-8
< Content-Length: 0
< Connection: keep-alive
< Access-Control-Allow-Origin: *
< Access-Control-Allow-Credentials: true
<
* Connection #0 to host httpbin.org left intact
Junades-MacBook-Pro-2:~ junade$ ▯
```

While GET requests merely show an existing resource, POST requests allow us to modify and update a resource. PUT requests instead allow us to create a new resource or override one, but specifically at a given endpoint.

What's the difference? PUT is idempotent, while POST is not idempotent. A PUT is like setting a variable, $x = 3$. You can do it over and over again, but the output is the same, x is 3.

POST is, instead, a lot like running $x++$; it causes a change that is not idempotent, the same way as $x++$ can't be repeated over and over to give the same exact variable. POST updates a resource, adds a subsidiary resource, or causes a change. PUT is instead used when you know the URL you want to create.

POST can be used to create when you know the URL of the factory that creates the resource for you.

So, for example, if the endpoint/user wants to generate a user account with a unique ID, we would use this:

```
POST /user
```

But if we wanted to create a user account at a particular endpoint, we would use `PUT`:

```
PUT /user/tom
```

Similarly, if we want to overwrite `tom` at the given endpoint, we can put another `PUT` request there:

```
PUT /user/tom
```

But suppose we don't know Tom's endpoint; instead, we just want to `PUT` to an endpoint with a user ID argument and some information will be updated:

```
POST /user
```

Hopefully that makes sense!

Now let's take a look at a given `HTTP POST` request.

We can create a request using URL encoded data:

```
curl --data "user=tom&manager=bob" https://httpbin.org/post
```

Note that if we specify data but not a request type in `curl` it will default to `POST`.

If we execute this, you can see the `Content-Type` is `x-www-form-urlencoded`:

```
                          junade — ·bash — 80×24
Junades-MacBook-Pro-2:~ junade$ curl --data "user=tom&manager=bob" https://httpb
in.org/post
{
  "args": {},
  "data": "",
  "files": {},
  "form": {
    "manager": "bob",
    "user": "tom"
  },
  "headers": {
    "Accept": "*/*",
    "Content-Length": "20",
    "Content-Type": "application/x-www-form-urlencoded",
    "Host": "httpbin.org",
    "User-Agent": "curl/7.43.0"
  },
  "json": null,
  "origin": "185.122.0.240",
  "url": "https://httpbin.org/post"
}
Junades-MacBook-Pro-2:~ junade$ 
```

However, we can also submit JSON data to the endpoint if the API allows us to and accepts that format:

```
curl -H "Content-Type: application/json" -X POST -d
'{"user":"tom","manager":"bob"}' https://httpbin.org/post
```

This provides the following output, noting the `Content-Type` is now JSON instead of `x-www-form-urlencoded` form it was before:

```
Last login: Sun Jul 10 23:14:11 on ttys006
[Junades-MacBook-Pro-2:~ junade$ curl -H "Content-Type: application/json" -X POST]
 -d '{"user":"tom","manager":"bob"}' https://httpbin.org/post
{
  "args": {},
  "data": "{\"user\":\"tom\",\"manager\":\"bob\"}",
  "files": {},
  "form": {},
  "headers": {
    "Accept": "*/*",
    "Content-Length": "30",
    "Content-Type": "application/json",
    "Host": "httpbin.org",
    "User-Agent": "curl/7.43.0"
  },
  "json": {
    "manager": "bob",
    "user": "tom"
  },
  "origin": "185.122.0.240",
  "url": "https://httpbin.org/post"
}
Junades-MacBook-Pro-2:~ junade$ 
```

We can now make a HTTP request using `PUT` by sending the same data to the `/put` endpoint:

```
curl -H "Content-Type: application/json" -X PUT -d
'{"user":"tom","manager":"bob"}' https://httpbin.org/put
```

Let's change the request type over to PUT:

```
                          🏠 junade — -bash — 80×24
Last login: Sun Jul 10 23:16:03 on ttys006
[Junades-MacBook-Pro-2:~ junade$ curl -H "Content-Type: application/json" -X PUT ]
-d '{"user":"tom","manager":"bob"}' https://httpbin.org/put
{
  "args": {},
  "data": "{\"user\":\"tom\",\"manager\":\"bob\"}",
  "files": {},
  "form": {},
  "headers": {
    "Accept": "*/*",
    "Content-Length": "30",
    "Content-Type": "application/json",
    "Host": "httpbin.org",
    "User-Agent": "curl/7.43.0"
  },
  "json": {
    "manager": "bob",
    "user": "tom"
  },
  "origin": "185.122.0.240",
  "url": "https://httpbin.org/put"
}
Junades-MacBook-Pro-2:~ junade$ 
```

Let's make the same request to a DELETE endpoint using the following curl request (in this example, we will submit data):

```
curl -H "Content-Type: application/json" -X DELETE -d '{"user":"tom"}'
https://httpbin.org/delete
```

This has the following output:

```
                            junade — -bash — 80×24
Last login: Sun Jul 10 23:22:13 on ttys006
[Junades-MacBook-Pro-2:~ junade$ curl -H "Content-Type: application/json" -X DELE]
TE -d '{"user":"tom"}' https://httpbin.org/delete
{
  "args": {},
  "data": "{\"user\":\"tom\"}",
  "files": {},
  "form": {},
  "headers": {
    "Accept": "*/*",
    "Content-Length": "14",
    "Content-Type": "application/json",
    "Host": "httpbin.org",
    "User-Agent": "curl/7.43.0"
  },
  "json": {
    "user": "tom"
  },
  "origin": "185.122.0.240",
  "url": "https://httpbin.org/delete"
}
Junades-MacBook-Pro-2:~ junade$ []
```

In the real world, you might not necessarily need to submit back any information related to the fact we've just deleted a resource (that's what DELETE is for). Instead, we may simply want to submit a 204 No Content message. Typically, I would not pass a message back.

HTTP/2 at a high level maintains this request structure. Remember that most HTTP/2 implementations require TLS (h2) and most browsers do not support HTTP/2 over cleartext (h2c), even though it is de facto possible in the RFC standard. If using HTTP/2 you realistically need TLS encryption on the request.

Woo! That was a mouthful, but that is everything you will need to know about an HTTP request, at a very high level. We didn't go into network detail, but this understanding is necessary for API architecture.

Now that we have a good understanding of HTTP requests and the methods used in HTTP communication, we can move on to understanding what makes an API RESTful.

RESTful API design

Many developers use and build REST APIs without understanding what makes them RESTful. So what actually is *REpresentational State Transfer*? Moreover, why is it important that an API is *RESTful*?

There are some key architectural constraints to an API being RESTful, the first of these is being stateless in nature.

Stateless nature

RESTful APIs are stateless; the client's context is not stored on the server between requests.

Suppose you create a basic PHP app that has login functionality. After validating the user credentials that are put into the login form, you may then go ahead and use a session to store a state of the logged in user as they proceed to their next state to carry out the next task.

This is unacceptable when it comes to a REST API; REST is a stateless protocol. The *ST* in REST stand for *State Transfer*; the state of a request should be transferred around rather than merely stored on the server. By transferring sessions instead of storing them you avoid having *sticky sessions* or *session affinity*.

In order for this to be implemented well the HTTP request happens in total isolation. Everything the server needs to carry out a GET, POST, PUT, or DELETE request is in the HTTP request itself. The server never relies on information from a previous request.

What are the benefits of doing this? Well, firstly it scales so much better; the most obvious benefit is that you don't need to store sessions on the server at all. This comes with additional functionalities too, when you put your API webservers behind a load balancer.

Clustering is difficult; clustering a web server with states either means you need to have sticky load balancing or you need to have a common store when it comes to sessions.

Versioning

Version your API, you will need to make changes and you don't want them breaking your client implementations. This can be done either using headers or in a URL itself. For example instead of /api/resource.json, you can have space for a version tag such as /api/v1/resource.json.

You can also implement the `HTTP Accept` header to perform this behavior or even put in place your own header. The client could send a request with the `API-Version` header set to 2 and the server will know to communicate to the client using version 2 of the API.

Filtering

Using a parameter query, we can filter a given by using a parameter. If we're dealing with an ordering system on the `/orders` endpoint, it is fairly easy to implement basic filtering.

Here, we filter for open orders using the `state` parameter:

```
GET /orders?state=open
```

Sorting

We can also add a `sort` parameter to sort by field. The `sort` field in turn contains a list of comma separated columns to sort on; the first in the list is the highest sort priority. In order to negatively sort you prefix a column with a negative sign –

- `GET /tickets?sort=-amount`: sort orders by descending order of amount (highest first).
- `GET /tickets?sort=-amount,created_at`: sort orders by descending order of amount (highest first). Within those amounts (with orders of equal amounts), older orders are listed first.

Searching

We can then search using a simple parameter that applies a search query that can then be routed through a search service (for example, ElasticSearch).

Suppose we want to search orders for the phrase refund, we can define a field for search queries:

```
GET /orders?q=refund
```

Limiting fields

Additionally, using a `fields` parameter we can query for specific fields:

```
GET /orders?fields=amount,created_at,customer_name,shipping_address
```

Returning new fields

A `PUT`, `POST`, or `PATCH` can change other criteria than the fields we update. This might be new timestamps or newly generated IDs. Accordingly, we should return the new resource representation on update.

In a `POST` request that has created a resource, you can send an `HTTP 201 CREATED` message back, alongside a `Location` header that points to the resource.

When in doubt – KISS

KISS is an acronym for **Keep it simple, stupid**.

The KISS principle states that most systems work best if they are kept simple rather than complicated. Throughout your programming journey, it is vital that this principle in mind.

Deciding to write a program with some predefined design patterns is often a poor idea. Code should never be forced into patterns. While writing code for a design pattern may work for a *Hello World* demonstration pattern, it doesn't usually work well the other way around.

Design patterns exist to resolve common recurring problems in code. It is vital they are used to address problems and not implemented where no such problems actually exist. By keeping your code as simple as possible and reducing the complexity of the overall program you are able to reduce the chance of failure.

The British Computer Society has published advice called *Senior Management in IT Projects* demonstrating that it is vital that the project, people, benefit, complexity, and progress are all thoroughly understood; beyond this, it is vital the project is fully understood upfront. Why is the project being completed? What are the risks? What is the recovery mechanism should the project derail?

Complex systems must handle errors gracefully to be robust. Redundancy must be balanced with complexity.

Software development life cycle

This chart is an open source diagram that describes the steps of software development:

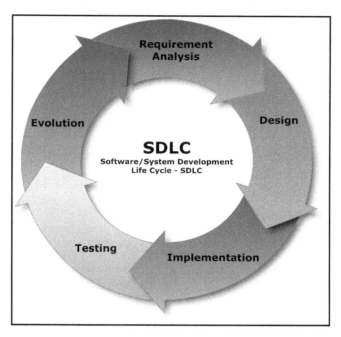

There are many different types of process to produce software, but all must contain the steps shown in the chart as they are fundamental to the software engineering process.

While nowadays it almost universally agreed that waterfall software engineering methodologies are no longer fit for purpose, the Agile counterparts that replace it still require some design (albeit smaller and more iterative) alongside strong testing practices.

It is vital that software development is not seen through a microscope and it's seen in the broader vision of software engineering.

On Scrum, and real Agility

Scrum is an iterative software development framework that claims to be Agile, based on the process published by the Scrum Alliance. It is graphed out as follows:

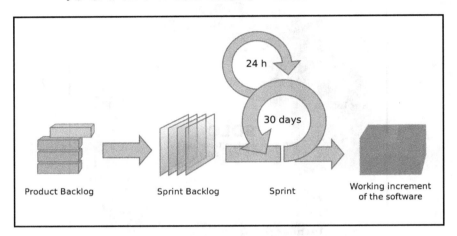

Many of us see the disasters left by the Certified Scrum Masters within software development teams, who largely use Agile as a buzzword to deliver some simply inane processes for writing software.

The Agile manifesto starts with the words, *individuals and interactions over processes and tools*. Scrum is a process, and a tightly defined process at that. Scrum is often implemented in a way where the development process is emphasized over the team. If there is one takeaway from this section, remember the phrase *people over processes*. If you choose to implement Scrum, you must be willing to adapt and change its processes to cope with change.

The whole point of Agile is to be agile; we want to adapt to changing requirements rapidly. We want flexibility, we don't want a tightly defined process that restricts us from adapting to rapidly changing requirements.

Filling in a time sheet, a purchase order, and dealing with bureaucratic governance processes do not help put software in customers' hands, so it has to be made as light as possible if it cannot go.

Time sheets are the perfect idea of something that is entirely wasteful. They are simply used to monitor developer performance, though in some those in management will pretend they have some magical agile benefit. They certainly will not help you make better software estimations, in any regard; Agile environments should seek to use projections over predictions.

I've seen Scrum Masters who endlessly repeat the quote: *no battle plan ever survives contact with the enemy*; while simultaneously enforcing rigid prediction schemes.

Accurate predictions are an oxymoron in the real world. You can't predict accurately for things that aren't certain, and in almost all cases, developers won't know the systems they are dealing with fully enough. Moreover, they don't know their own personal efficiency from day to day; it just can't be foreseen accurately.

I've even encountered environments where these strict predictions (often not even made by the developers themselves) are enforced by strict disciplinary procedures.

Reducing complexity by dividing problems and addressing them in small chunks is great practice; reducing your huge teams of programmers into smaller teams is also amazing practice.

Between the systems that developers are building in these small teams (commonly known as *tribes*), a system architect is often needed to ensure there is consistency between the teams.

Spotify use this tribe architecture to develop software; indeed, I would highly recommend reading the paper *Scaling Agile @ Spotify with Tribes, Squads, Chapters & Guilds* by Henrik Kniberg and Anders Ivarsson.

This system architect ensures there is consistency between all the different services that are built.

Turning to specifically Scrum, Scrum is an Agile process. The Scrum Guide (yes, it is even a trademark) defines the rules of Scrum in a 16-page document.

Agile, however, contains many different processes alongside many other methodologies; Agile is a very broad knowledge base.

Scrum Masters like to pretend Agile happens in an isolated environment in a development team. This is far from the truth; the entire organization structure plays into Scrum.

Extreme Programming (**XP**) is a very broad process and it is largely understood the interactions between these processes. By cherry-picking these processes, you end up with an ineffective process; this is why Scrum struggles.

Requirements change; this includes them changing mid-Sprint. When Scrum Masters insist on no changes after a Sprint has started, which leaves the team more ineffective to respond to real change.

When developing in an Agile mechanism, we must remember that our software must be resilient enough to cope with the ever-changing requirements (resulting in ever-changing software design). Your software architecture must be able to cope with the stress of change. It is therefore vital that developers also understand and engage with the technical processes required to achieve software resilient enough to cope with the pace of change.

Companies that can't be flexible and respond to change are less effective than those who can; accordingly, they have a significant edge in the business world. When picking a company, them being Agile is not merely about the quality of the job you do but it is also vital to your job security.

My message is simple here; take technical practices seriously when implementing a process, and remember not to blindly follow obscene processes as it can harm an entire business.

Developers shouldn't be treated like children. If they can't code or write bad code they can't continue to be employed as developers.

In essence, in order to manage risk, it's best to look at your backlog and use historical progress to create projections as to where your project will be. The role of the manager should be to take away obstacles that stop developers doing their jobs.

Finally, if you ever are in a team with a Scrum Master with a terrible understanding of software development (and Agile for that matter), remind them strongly that people must come above process and that true agility is aided by code that can withstand the stresses of change.

Scrum Masters will sometimes will argue that Agile means no upfront design. This is untrue, Agile means no *big* upfront design.

You need to sack people sometimes

I have worked in development environments where managers are too scared to sack, they either just torture developers by punishing them for a job they evidently can't do by trying to put perverse restrictions on development teams or let them wreak havoc on the development processes.

Talented developers get disillusioned by the production of bad code or the unequal skill-basis. Other developers get away with poor code when they are often forced into a maintenance nightmare. Faced with the prospect of a maintenance nightmare (or in all likelihood, an increasing maintenance nightmare), they then resign.

Alternatively, the restrictive work conditions imposed to compensate for bad developers disillusion talented developers. Sick of being treated like idiots (because the other developers are idiots), they then take a job offer at a far better firm that offers them far better career prospects, and a better working environment with happier, more talented staff. They accept this offer as the company they are moving to will probably also have better business prospects and better compensation alongside happier engineers in a better work environment.

There is one more extreme to this scenario; the business gains such an adverse reputation they cannot hire permanent developers; they then pay exorbitant fees for expensive contract developers while taking chances on their skillsets. While hemorrhaging money on contract developers, the business out of desperation will then probably pick up anyone who is willing to work on these projects. Interviewers of these developers will probably have not asked the right questions for the systems they will be building, leading to a big gamble on the quality of contractors being hired. The company decreases its chances of hiring good permanent staff, and the business enters tailspin as the company's demise gets worse. I have seen this exact scenario multiple times; each time the company has faced a slow and painful recession. If you are ever invited to work for a company which is similar to this, I strongly advise you to look elsewhere, unless you truly believe you are able to bring reform to such an organization.

If you ever take a management job in an organization such as this, ensure you have the powers to make meaningful change, the powers to hire the right people and fire the wrong people. If not, your tenure at such an organization will merely be spent trying to shift the deckchairs while suffering from a high staff churn rate.

Talented staff can be trusted; those passionate about what they are doing will not need restrictions to prevent them from slacking off.

If there are talented staff who can't perform their duties, it is highly unlikely your developers are merely slackers; you need to remove the bureaucratic processes that are restrictions to development.

Compulsively performing rituals that add nothing to putting software in users' hands adds nothing of value to the development team.

Lean project management

Lean project management allows you to regularly deliver business value without being based on lists of requirements, features, and functions.

The book *The Machine That Changed the World* was based on the Massachusetts Institute of Technology's $5 million 5-year study on the automotive industry, making the term lean production world famous.

This book proposed the following principles of lean:

- Identify customers and specify values
- Identify and map the value stream
- Create flow by eliminating waste
- Respond to customer pull
- Persue perfection

From this, there are the following Lean Principles when it comes to software development, which are largely based on the manufacturing principles of lean production:

- Eliminate waste
- Amplify learning
- Decide as late as possible
- Deliver as fast as possible
- Empower the team
- Build integrity in
- See the whole

Good architecture through reusable components, automated deployments, and good architecture can all assist in attaining this goal.

YAGNI and defering decisions

You aren't going to need it – you don't need to add functionality until it's necessary. Only add things that are vital to the success of your project. You probably won't need a lot of functionality for the first version of your web app; it's best to defer this until necessary.

By deferring unnecessary functionality, you are able to keep your software design as simple as it needs to be. This helps you cope with the pace of change. Later in the software development process you will be more educated regarding the requirements, and more importantly, your client will have a more precise projection as to where they want the product to head.

When you make decisions on software later, you have more data and more education. Some decisions have to be made upfront, but if you can defer them, that's often a good idea.

Monitoring

Monitoring systems become critical as you scale. Effective monitoring can drastically ease the maintenance of services.

Having spoken to multiple experts in this field, this is the advice I have collected on the subject:

- Choose your key statistics carefully. Users don't care if your machine is low on CPU but they do care if your API is slow.
- Use aggregators; think about services, not machines. If you have more than a handful of machines, you should treat them as an amorphous blob.
- Avoid the Wall of Graphs. They are slow and it's information overload for a human. Each dashboard should have five graphs with no more than five lines per graphs.
- Quantiles aren't aggregable, they're hard to get meaningful information from. However, averages are easy to reason. A response time of 10 ms in the first quartile isn't really useful as information, but a 400 ms average response time shows a clear problem that needs to be addressed.
- In addition to this, averages are far easier to calculate than quantiles. They are computationally easy, and especially useful as soon as you need scale the monitoring system.
- Monitoring has a cost. Consider whether the resources are really worth it. Is a 1 second monitoring frequency really better than 10 second monitoring? Is the cost worth it? Monitoring isn't free, it has a computational cost.
- That said, the Nyquist-Shannon sampling theorem demonstrates that if you sample every 20 seconds you can't reconstruct patterns at 10 seconds apart. Let's suppose there is a service that is crashing or reducing the speed of your computer system every 10 seconds – it can't be detected. Bear this in mind throughout your data analysis process.

- Correlation not causation – beware of conformation bias. Be sure to achieve a formal relationship of what is causing a particular issue before doing anything drastic.
- Both logs and metrics are good. Logs let you figure out details, metrics give you the high level.
- Have a way to deal with non-critical alerts. What do you do with all those 404 errors in your web server log files?
- Remember the KISS principle mentioned earlier; keep your monitoring as simple as possible.

Tests fight legacy

Automated tests are the best tool to fight legacy code.

By having automated tests such as unit tests or behavioral tests, you are able to refactor legacy code effectively with confidence that little can be broken.

Badly written systems often consist of tightly coupled functions. One change to a function in one class may well break a function in a completely different class, leading to a domino effect of more classes being broken until the entire application is broken.

In order to decouple classes and follow practices such as the Single Responsibility Principle, refactoring must be carried out. Any refactoring effort must be sure not to break code elsewhere in an application.

This brings us onto the topic of test coverage: is it a truly meaningful figure?

Alberto Savoia answered this question best in an amusing anecdote he placed online on artima.com; let's take a read:

> *Early one morning, a programmer asked the great master: "I am ready to write some unit tests. What code coverage should I aim for?"*
> *The great master replied: "Don't worry about coverage, just write some good tests."*
> *The programmer smiled, bowed, and left.*
> *...*
> *Later that day, a second programmer asked the same question. The great master pointed at a pot of boiling water and said: "How many grains of rice should I put in that pot?"*
> *The programmer, looking puzzled, replied: "How can I possibly tell you? It depends on how many people you need to feed, how hungry they are, what other food you are serving, how much rice you have available, and so on."*

"Exactly," said the great master.

The second programmer smiled, bowed, and left.

…

Toward the end of the day, a third programmer came and asked the same question about code coverage.

"Eighty percent and no less!" Replied the master in a stern voice, pounding his fist on the table.

The third programmer smiled, bowed, and left.

…

After this last reply, a young apprentice approached the great master:

"Great master, today I overheard you answer the same question about code coverage with three different answers. Why?"

The great master stood up from his chair: "Come get some fresh tea with me and let's talk about it."

After they filled their cups with smoking hot green tea, the great master began to answer: "The first programmer is new and just getting started with testing. Right now he has a lot of code and no tests. He has a long way to go; focusing on code coverage at this time would be depressing and quite useless. He's better off just getting used to writing and running some tests. He can worry about coverage later."

"The second programmer, on the other hand, is quite experienced both at programming and testing. When I replied by asking her how many grains of rice I should put in a pot, I helped her realize that the amount of testing necessary depends on a number of factors, and she knows those factors better than I do – it's her code after all. There is no single, simple, answer, and she's smart enough to handle the truth and work with that."

"I see," said the young apprentice, "but if there is no single simple answer, then why did you answer the third programmer 'Eighty percent and no less'?"

The great master laughed so hard and loud that his belly, evidence that he drank more than just green tea, flopped up and down.

"The third programmer wants only simple answers – even when there are no simple answers … and then does not follow them anyway."

The young apprentice and the grizzled great master finished drinking their tea in contemplative silence.

Alberto is portraying a simple message: focusing on having as much business logic and functionality is the best way forward. Test coverage is not something you should follow an arbitrary figure for.

There are things which it makes sense not to test, and there are different logical paths even of code that has already been tested.

Moreover, in distributed systems the communication between APIs or systems can be what breaks the system. In distributed architectures, testing code may not be enough. Strong monitoring systems become vital. Infrastructure as code to ensure consistent deployments and upgrades comes to the foreground. Moreover, achieving loosely coupled services and proper inter-process communication is more beneficial to the overall architecture than some unit tests.

There is an alternative approach to Test-Driven Development (TDD). Behavior-Driven Development (BDD) provides us a different mechanism of testing our code; let's discuss it.

Behavior-Driven Development

BDD works by implementing tests using human-readable stories.

Cucumber is a tool that implements a BDD workflow by using human-readable feature files written in plain English language, for example:

```
Feature: Log in to site.
  In order to see my profile
    As a user
    I need to log-in to the site.

Scenario: Logs in to the site
  Given I am on "/"
  When I follow "Log In"
    And I fill in "Username" with "admin"
    And I fill in "Password" with "test"
    And I press "Log in"
  Then I should see "Log out"
    And I should see "My account"
```

Now, this section is going to be an incredibly simple exploration of Behat to pique your curiosity. If you want to learn more, please head to http://www.behat.org.

The Behat guide contains an example of a user story for the ls command. It's quite a respectable example, so here it is:

```
Feature: ls
  In order to see the directory structure
  As a UNIX user
  I need to be able to list the current directory's contents

  Scenario: List 2 files in a directory
    Given I am in a directory "test"
```

```
And I have a file named "foo"
And I have a file named "bar"
When I run "ls"
Then I should get:
  """
  bar
  foo
  """
```

In order to install Behat, you can amend your `composer.json` file so that it is required in your development environments:

```
{
  "require-dev": {
    "behat/behat": "~2.5"
  },
  "config": {
    "bin-dir": "bin/"
  }
}
```

This will install Behat version 2.5, there is also Behat version 3, which contains a whole suite of new features without losing too much backward compatibility. That said, many projects out there are still utilizing Behat 2.

Then you can run Behat using the following command:

bin/behat

We get the following output:

By using the init flag we can then create a features directory with some basic information to get us started:

```
 junade — root@junade-test: ~/behat — ssh root@178.62.40.19 — 80×24
[root@junade-test:~/behat# bin/behat --init
+d features - place your *.feature files here
+d features/bootstrap - place bootstrap scripts and static files here
+f features/bootstrap/FeatureContext.php - place your feature related code here
root@junade-test:~/behat#
```

Accordingly, let's write our `feature/ls.feature` file with the following feature and scenario, as follows:

```
 junade — root@junade-test: ~/behat — ssh root@178.62.40.19 — 80×24
Feature: ls
    In order to see the directory structure
    As a UNIX user
    I need to be able to list the current directory's contents

Scenario: List 2 files in a directory
    Given I am in a directory "test"
    And I have a file named "foo"
    And I have a file named "bar"
    When I run "ls"
    Then I should get:
        """

        bar
        foo
        """
~
~
~
~
~
~
~
"features/ls.feature" 15L, 341C                              1,1            All
```

If we now run Behat we'll find the following output:

Behat accordingly returns some code snippets so we can implement the undefined steps:

```
/**
 * @Given /^I am in a directory "([^"]*)"$/
 */
public function iAmInADirectory($arg1)
{
  throw new PendingException();
}

/**
 * @Given /^I have a file named "([^"]*)"$/
 */
public function iHaveAFileNamed($arg1)
```

```
{
    throw new PendingException();
}

/**
 * @When /^I run "([^"]*)"$/
 */
public function iRun($arg1)
{
    throw new PendingException();
}

/**
 * @Then /^I should get:$/
 */
public function iShouldGet(PyStringNode $string)
{
    throw new PendingException();
}
```

Now, in the feature directory that was created for us is a bootstrap folder that contains a `FeatureContext.php` file. Within this file, you will be able to find the body of your class:

You may have noticed this block in the class body. We can put the generated methods here:

```
//
// Place your definition and hook methods here:
//
//   /**
//    * @Given /^I have done something with "([^"]*)"$/
//    */
//   public function iHaveDoneSomethingWith($argument)
//   {
//     doSomethingWith($argument);
//   }
//
```

I've done this as follows:

You may notice the body is full of `PendingException` messages. We need to replace these bodies with the actual functionality; fortunately, the Behat documentation contains functions with these methods populated:

```php
/** @Given /^I am in a directory "([^"]*)"$/ */
public function iAmInADirectory($dir)
{
  if (!file_exists($dir)) {
    mkdir($dir);
  }
  chdir($dir);
}

/** @Given /^I have a file named "([^"]*)"$/ */
public function iHaveAFileNamed($file)
{
  touch($file);
}

/** @When /^I run "([^"]*)"$/ */
public function iRun($command)
{
  exec($command, $output);
  $this->output = trim(implode("\n", $output));
}

/** @Then /^I should get:$/ */
public function iShouldGet(PyStringNode $string)
{
  if ((string) $string !== $this->output) {
    throw new Exception(
      "Actual output is:\n" . $this->output
    );
  }
}
```

Now we can run Behat and we should see our scenario and its various steps completed:

```
[root@junade-test:~/behat# bin/behat
Feature: ls
  In order to see the directory structure
  As a UNIX user
  I need to be able to list the current directory's contents

  Scenario: List 2 files in a directory    # features/ls.feature:6
    Given I am in a directory "test"        # FeatureContext::iAmInADirectory()
    And I have a file named "foo"           # FeatureContext::iHaveAFileNamed()
    And I have a file named "bar"           # FeatureContext::iHaveAFileNamed()
    When I run "ls"                         # FeatureContext::iRun()
    Then I should get:                      # FeatureContext::iShouldGet()
      """

      bar
      foo
      """

1 scenario (1 passed)
5 steps (5 passed)
0m0.011s
root@junade-test:~/behat# []
```

By using Mink with Behat we are able to accordingly use Selenium to run browser tests. Selenium will spin up a browser using Mink and we can then run Behat tests in the browser.

Summary

In this chapter, I've sought to tie up some loose ends. We've discussed some of the networking side of web development by learning about HTTP. In addition to this, we've learned about how RESTful APIs can be effectively designed.

This book is now coming to an end; let's revisit some core values that make our code great:

- Favor composition over inheritance
- Avoid repetitive coding (the DRY principle means Don't Repeat Yourself)
- Keep It Simple, Stupid
- Don't use design patterns just for using design patterns, introduce design patterns when you identify a recurring issue that they can solve
- Abstraction is awesome, interfaces help you abstract
- Write code in line with good standards

- Separate responsibilities throughout your code
- Use dependency management and dependency injection; Composer is now available
- Tests save development time; they are critical for any refactoring effort and reduce breakages

Thank you for making it through this book; this book is a collection of my rants about software development; having had an incredibly diverse career, there are many lessons I have learned brutally and lot of eyesore code I have had to refactor. I have seen some of the worst, but also been a part of some of the most exciting PHP projects around. I hope in this book I have been able to share some of my experiences in this field.

It is easy for developers to hide themselves away from the reality of development; there are few people who know best practices when it comes to software design and architecture, and a very limited set of those choose PHP as their development language of choice.

For many of us, the code we produce is more than a hobby or a job, it is the limit of our expression as software engineers. Accordingly, writing it in a poetic, expressive, and a lasting fashion is our duty.

Think about the code you would love to maintain; that is the code you have a duty to produce. Minimalism, reducing complexity, and separating concerns are key to achieving this.

Computer science may be grounded in mathematics and theorems, but our code sits above this. By utilizing the basis of a Turing complete language we are able to write code that is creative and functional.

This locates software engineering in an odd vacuum compared to many other disciplines; while being very metricized, it also must be appealing to humans. I hope this book has helped you achieve these ends.

Index

www.ingramcontent.com/pod-product-compliance
Lightning Source LLC
Chambersburg PA
CBHW060532060326
40690CB00017B/3463